Clothed with Strength

Single Women Serving Christ in the Arab World

Christine Ford McLaren

Published for Christine Ford McLaren by Verité CM Limited,
124 Sea Place, Worthing, West Sussex BN12 4BG
+44 (0) 1903 241975

email: enquiries@veritecm.com
www.veritecm.com

British Library Cataloguing in Publication Data

A catalogue record for this book is available from
the British Library

ISBN: 978-1-914388-60-6

Scripture quotations are taken from the The Holy Bible,
English Standard Version® (ESV®) © 2001 by Crossway, a publishing
ministry of Good News Publishers. All rights reserved.

Design and Print Management by Verité CM Ltd
www.veritecm.com

She dresses herself with strength
And makes her arms strong.
Proverbs 31:17

I know how to be brought low, and I know how to abound.
In any and every circumstance, I have learned the secret
of facing plenty and hunger, abundance and need. I can
do all things through him who strengthens me.
Phil 4:12-13

In you I am complete.
Let my life bear witness
That you are enough
Always enough
More than enough.
Liz Snell
A Liturgy for a Single Person Going to Church
Every Moment Holy, Volume III: The Work of the People.

Commendations

'Bold, adventurous, and indefatigable are just a few of the words to describe the six women whose lives Christine Ford McLaren spotlights in this highly readable and compelling book! History comes to life as these fearless single women follow God's call into incredibly challenging situations. Though focused on unmarried women, this book is a must for both marrieds and singles—as well as women and men, interested in learning what it means to live faithful, fruitful lives in Muslim contexts.'

Dr Gail Schlosser
Assistant Director of The Lilias Trotter Center

'Single women have been a force for the gospel in the Middle East for well over a century, and if you are interested in their stories, then this book is for you. This well-researched book will take you through deserts, cities, and the back of pickup trucks as you read how six women lived out sacrificial love for the people around them. Each woman had their own unique calling in serving the Lord, and I'm confident you will find encouragement as you read their biographies.'

Josh Perkins
Cross-cultural trainer, Bible teacher, and educator

'The advance of the message of the gospel in Muslim societies is complex and multi-layered. Only the most prominent actors appear in the histories--names like John of Damascus, Timothy I, Francis of Assisi and Samuel Zwemer. That is why I was delighted to read Christine Ford McLaren's work including some names I had never heard before. The list includes Fanny Lutton, Sarah Hosmon, Hazel St John, Ada and Ida Stoltzfaus. There was one name I had heard before—Aileen Coleman. In fact I heard about Aileen a few days previous to writing these lines. She was awarded a special medal of achievement by the King of Jordan. I was delighted to watch a short video of her receiving the honor at 91 years of age. Despite Aileen's well-deserved recognition, the names in this list are not the famous heroes of Christian mission to Islam. They all share a few characteristics: they are women, they are unmarried and they served as representatives of Christ among Muslims. Because Jesus told his followers that the last shall be first, it is important that we consider these unsung heroes who have much to teach us about serving Christ. Christine has unearthed their history, portraying them for us as real people with real struggles and admirable perseverance. Though she's now married, Christine herself has experienced the demands of ministry in the Muslim world as a single woman. Her insight into these women and their experience is a significant addition to the history of Christian mission. It is an addition that few have considered—the enormous contribution of single women to outreach and mission among Muslims. Read it and be inspired by a few humble women who simply kept obeying their Lord even when the cost was high.'

Michael Kuhn, Ph.D.
Director, International Theological Education Network

Contents

Foreword

Who better qualified than Christine Ford McLaren to address the topic: Single Women Missionaries in the Arab world? Married now for sixteen years, she spent twenty-one years as a single in ministry – serving in the Arab world in various roles. She has experienced first hand, up close and personal, the assumptions and prejudices, the joys and the challenges as a single woman in a culture where marriage status infers value. Now, as a married woman, she brings understanding, empathy and perspective to the unique experience of a single woman in this particular role and place.

This book is for the single woman who has left home, family and culture to minister in a land foreign to her. It is also for those who promise to pray, pledge financial support toward her mission, have an admiration for her so-called 'life of sacrifice' but limited understanding of what she and her colleagues face simply by virtue of being single. Single in the Arab world.

Woman missionaries are part of my spiritual DNA. As a child I thrilled to the stories of real-life women who spoke at our annual church mission conferences. I read and relished the adventures of Patricia St. John, Amy Carmichael, Isabel Kuhn, Elisabeth Elliot as well as other notables in books, articles and collections about women missionaries. Then I 'met' Lilias Trotter who has claimed, to varying degrees, four decades of my life. Through Lilias I met Christine – her husband Alasdair being partner in research and point-person for all things Lilias.

One might ask: Why one more book? What distinguishes this work from other missionary biographies? Until I read this book, I had never made a distinction between single and married women in missions. The author's Introduction alone was enough to convince: there is a difference. There is a difference both in what the single woman perceives/experiences – at home and on foreign terrain - and how, in turn, she is perceived/experienced. The Introduction is worth the price of the book!

Yet this book is more than that. It is a collection of stories of six women who have changed a particular part of the world – the Arab world – by their very presence: coming alongside nationals, entering into their lives, in all manner of ways, while sharing the Good News of the gospel. Through Christine's gifted storytelling we glimpse their hearts, their love, their sacrifice. We witness how they pioneered ways and means to reach the souls of individuals thirsty for truth and a better way of life. These women come alive, real down-to-earth people, as Christine relates their stories with her unique blend of candor, humor and integrity. She follows these inspirational stories with the experiences of eight contemporary women - the Current Crop - who, in conclusion, relate their own challenges (and advantages) of being single missionaries to the Arab world in the here-and-now.

For those of us who have different callings, we might lament: What am I doing with my life? We might be intimidated, in comparison, by our own limited world and work. Yet as doors are opened into the lives and hearts of these fourteen remarkable women, spiritual insight is proffered which transcends place or gender or marital status. Christine has provided a great service while taking us through the joys and challenges of these women, transcending the particulars with universal truths on how to live – whatever our calling – in union with Christ, growing ever into His likeness.

Take and read! Examine your understanding of commitment! Embrace God's call for your life!

Miriam Hoffman Rockness

Introduction

'Are you sure you don't mind going overseas single?'

After being asked for the fifth time, I was ready: I would be okay if you would stop reminding me.

I was preparing to embark on a missionary career in the Middle East. During the vetting process, I underwent interviews, filled in forms, and was repeatedly asked about my marital status.

In my heart, I did want to marry and have children. Yet, the Lord was beckoning me. While I was heading for the Arab world, a friend said, 'Now, don't go and get married.' I knew several women who were heading overseas, but met nice men, married, and stayed home. Paul wished that all could remain single (1 Cor 7:7–8), and Jesus said to go and make disciples of all nations (Mt 28). My main motivation to go overseas as a missionary was God's call on my life, fanned by the lack of Christian witness among those who knew little or nothing about the person and work of Christ.

After spending nearly forty years in and around the Arab world, I have gained some insight into Arab culture. Sometimes I wonder what my Arab friends and neighbours really thought. I flew to the Middle East on my own and visited Europe during the summer. Their young women were kept close and their movements were monitored by family members. All for good intentions—in their culture, the honour of the family depends on the behaviour of its women.

The questions did not let up when I went to Jordan to study Arabic. Many Arab neighbours asked when I would marry. I vowed I was waiting for a man who was *mustaqeem* (upright, seeking the right path). One said I should abandon this ideal and just marry someone, while another offered her taxi-driving brother. One of my teammates in Cairo mused that I was working in that great city until a knight came along and swept me away. Even back in Toronto for a visit, a friend resolved I should stay in Ontario and marry.

One year I was invited to present a seminar for singles at a conference for women involved in ministry to Muslims. My seminar was to focus on loneliness and sexual purity. I declined, adding I did not feel I had triumphed in these areas. The organisers thought this was a great reason to come and share any struggles. They added I would need to pay for travel expenses, which I could not afford. No problem, they said, you do some fundraising and we will do some fundraising.

I found it tough to write that seminar and embrace Paul's commendation to remain single for the sake of the gospel. In the married cultures of the church, the Arab world and the media, the Lord preserved the verse from 1 Corinthians for me. I began to treasure it.

Advantages

There are significant advantages to being a single missionary. I learned about the society firsthand, whereas my married friends tag-teamed with their husbands, preventing them from coming face-to-face with a male-dominated culture. One day the electricity went off in my flat perched atop one of Amman's nine hills. At that point, I was one of half a dozen single women missionaries on our team. My flatmate and I discovered we needed to pay an electricity bill which we had not seen. So, we found the correct office, waded through the smoky air and paid our bill. We were the only women and the only foreigners. But we learned how to pay an electricity bill.

We worked jobs and were out in society. Our married friends asked us where they could go for the evening as they led more cloistered lives. We had autonomy. We came and went as we pleased.

Disadvantages

While we had knowledge about paying electricity bills and using local currency, we would have been grateful for a husband to do these things for us. Without a family on site, we were on our own. I will forever be grateful for families in our mission who welcomed me day or night to be part of theirs. I slept on the floor and joined in whatever was going on.

Living in a segregated society meant we did not have access to men. A missionary who spent decades in Morocco said she missed having friendships with men, as her life revolved around her Moroccan women friends. Another missionary told me she welcomed single female missionaries to her home for a visit. When they arrived, she would encourage conversation between her husband and visitors. With the work we were doing, we sometimes had more in common with the husbands than the wives.

Some Consolation

When I first visited the Arab world on a summer team, one of the missionaries told us there were two roles for single women in the Arab world—nuns or prostitutes. Some years ago, I took a group of students to Egypt. I was chatting with an Egyptian woman on public transport when she cocked her head and asked, 'Are you a nun?' I smiled and replied in the negative, but was secretly pleased that I had fallen on that side of the single woman fence.

After two years in Jordan, I took a training course in Cairo to learn to teach English as a second language. The institute that trained me hired me, so I remained in Cairo for four years. Then, I relocated to the UK to work at our international office and learned British English. Six years later, I began work at our Canadian office, bought a house and settled down. Once I finished decorating it, an old friendship with a lovely British man warmed up and a year later, we married and I moved to England. Five years later after doing some fundraising, we moved to the Gulf for eight years. Being married meant I fit into an acceptable box in Arab culture. However, I was more constrained by domestic concerns. Between my husband and I, we have over one hundred years of being single. We retain a soft spot for singles and seek to support and encourage them, both informally and through mission conference seminars.

I have chosen in this book to highlight the lives of six feisty, single women who served the Lord for many years in the Arab world. Fanny Lutton's visits to the Shia *matam* echoed mine, except Fanny's visits did not involve a microphone. Sarah Hosmon's tales continue to impress, especially as they were done on a prosthetic leg. Hazel St John, whose story was a catalyst for this project, continues to inspire me. I was in Jordan at the same time that Ada and Ida Stoltzfus were not far away in Hebron. A neighbouring building to mine in Jordan was full of families with roots from that city. Aileen Coleman's bus trip to Syria caused me to recall my own regular visa runs to Damascus. Please allow me to introduce you to some of my new heroes.

Fanny Lutton

At first Fanny was 'pessimistic'. How could she learn this 'impossible' language, come alongside the people and their 'strange customs' and 'endure...let alone enjoy' the climate?[1] In time she was welcomed as a guest in the home of most Arab women in Muscat, present-day Oman.[2]

Beginnings, 1861–1902

Fanny was the youngest child of an Irish immigrant family, born in Sydney, Australia in 1861. As she was committed to caring for her parents, Fanny declined a marriage proposal from the son of a wealthy family. This choice of duty over comfort meant Fanny was later able to pursue overseas ministry.[3]

Fanny found work cleaning houses as well as tailoring garments. She was active at her church, St Peter's Anglican, Woolloomooloo. Fanny trained to become a deaconess and spoke on Sunday afternoons 'from a religious platform' in the Sydney Domain, a large park in the city. In connection with her church work, she received training as a midwife and nurse, which took her to a rough part of the city to work with the poor. Donning her deaconess' garb, she was not troubled and was even honoured.[4]

When Fanny was nearly thirty-seven, her parents died, which left her alone without a future in Sydney. She applied to the Church of England to become a missionary, but was too old—the cutoff age was thirty-five. Around that time, Samuel and Amy Zwemer were visiting Sydney, where Amy had also trained as a deaconess.[5] Samuel Zwemer had co-founded the Arabian Mission in 1889 and would later be known as the Apostle to Islam. After some discussions, Fanny, age forty-one, sailed away with the Zwemers, eventually landing in Bahrain where she assisted Amy with the Acorn School.[6]

Bahrain, 1902–1904

Two square holes served as windows under the low ceiling in the Acorn School for Muslim, Jewish, and Christian girls. The students wore everything from 'rag-tag' to 'velvet gowns embroidered with gold braid'. In time, packing crates were upgraded to chairs and school supplies sent from friends in the US proved helpful.[7]

On the walls of the Acorn School were painted Scripture scenes, including the raising of Lazarus. Amy and Fanny believed that, like Lazarus, Jesus would raise 'those who are spiritually dead on this island.' They prayed that their fledgling school would be like the yeast hidden in some flour until all the flour was leavened (Mt 13:33).[8]

School days began at eight with a prayer and a hymn, followed by lessons. The girls transcribed their memory work such as the Lord's Prayer or the days of creation. Some retained the hymns and Fanny overheard 'Jesus Loves Me' as the children drew water from the well. Lessons were held on three mornings and sewing on the other two. The girls stitched quilts and aprons and while proud of their new thimbles, soon reverted to bare fingers. Extra needles were stored in their noses, which were pierced.[9]

The teachers struggled without ventilation and closed the school during the three hottest months when daytime highs averaged around 40°C. It was 'uphill work' to gather the girls in the autumn, yet there were greater challenges. Many Muslim parents would prefer their children were dead rather than permit them to be educated in a Christian school. 'The enmity of the cross', wrote Fanny, 'is very bitter.'[10]

The children were raised with less discipline than Fanny was used to. It was easy to win their love and Fanny witnessed their quick response to any warmth shown to them as the girls looked up to extol their teacher's goodness.[11]

Local girls married young at that time and their husbands sometimes banned them from attending school. Fanny recounted the story of one ten-year-old who missed classes because her husband beat her and banned her from the school. Parents were keen for their daughters to marry, but there was no shame if they could not read.[12]

Busrah, 1904–1905

Besides working at the budding school, Fanny welcomed new arrivals to the mission station, including Miss Jennie Scardefield in 1903.[13] When Fanny formally joined the Arabian Mission in 1904, she and Jennie were posted to Busrah, southern port city in modern-day Iraq, for language study.[14] Jennie began full-time studies, but Fanny had enough Arabic to pass the first exam immediately, as she had 'lived privately' with missionaries in Bahrain.[15]

Learning to read, write, and speak Arabic in her forties was no mean feat. During a subsequent visit home to Australia, she amused her nephews and nieces by reading aloud to them from her Arabic Bible.[16]

In Busrah, an Arabian Mission team was involved in medical work. Fanny worked alongside her mission colleague Dr Worral, who was already working diligently with the women, besides running her women's clinic and responding to calls for assistance. All the while, Fanny studied for her Arabic examinations, which were increasingly difficult.[18] Fanny viewed Arabic acquisition as more about working hard and 'stick-to-it-iveness' than talent.[19]

Busrah provided Fanny with fewer opportunities than Bahrain. She arrived just as the summer heat descended, which diminished visits to women.[20] The climate was severe and Fanny learned not to behave as if she were in a more benign setting.[21] Also, she was not living in the midst of the people as she had done in Bahrain.[22] As Busrah was under Muslim Turkish rule, unlike Bahrain, this further curtailed mission work as the Ottomans forbade Christian evangelism.

Fanny found the Turkish women different from the Arabs in Bahrain:

> We were greeted with many compliments and salaams, and requested to enter and be seated. The room was fully furnished, with tables, chairs, cushions, etc., and the ladies of the house actually sitting on chairs. Cigarettes were first offered, and as we politely declined, we were then offered sweet sherbet and after that coffee in very tiny cups. Many questions were asked (it is not impolite to ask your business, your age, and all personal matters) and answered.[23]

Fanny did have openings to speak of her Christian faith. One of Dr Worrall's patients suffered from fluid retention. Fanny visited this patient often, who listened when the missionaries spoke of Christ. When the patient began to change the subject, Dr Worrall speculated the servants noticed her interest and alerted her against listening too closely.[24]

Fanny spoke to the female patients after morning prayers at the dispensary. 'I wish you could see their faces (and if you are a woman you have that privilege) and hear their responses,' wrote Fanny. She taught them a short prayer and the women all repeated it aloud.[25]

The challenges the missionaries faced were typical of those engaged in Christian ministry to Muslims. The doctrine of the atonement was wholly rejected by Mohammed, women refused to even touch the Bible and were more difficult to witness to than the men, recounted

Fanny. She prayed she would be worthy of the work and not damage the kingdom of God in the minds of those she met.[26]

Bahrain, 1905–1911

Back in Bahrain, Fanny assumed the mantle of women's work in the absence of Mrs Zwemer, who had moved to Egypt with her husband.[27] She conceded life was not 'romantic' or adventurous, but it was also not 'monotonous.'[28] She could enter homes and always find women with whom to read the Bible. She sometimes visited with Mrs Bennett, who wrote that they connected with all types of women whether well off or not. Mrs Bennett noted the women often asked Fanny to read the Bible to them, yet in the middle of talking about the Lord, one would motion to Fanny's brooch, asking if it was gold.[29]

Fanny witnessed a great contrast in the homes she visited. At one, they asked for the woman of the house, but were informed she had died the previous week from cholera. They were then led to a shed, where another elderly woman lying in squalor asked the missionaries for a prescription. Fanny returned with a doctor and washed the old woman. The on-looking neighbours then joined in to clean the hovel, remarking it had not been cleaned for twenty years.[30]

At the next house, one of the nine women asked what was in Fanny's handbag, so Fanny told them she had 'the Word of God—good news.' Another asked if it was the Koran, to which Fanny replied it was not, then added in the Koran, it was written that God sent the gospel to guide us. They all implored Fanny to read, which caused her to be thankful.[31]

Fanny visited a devout Muslim lady, who was literate. This lady was always careful to wash her hands before touching the Koran and knew why Fanny had travelled to Bahrain, yet always extended a welcome, remarking Fanny's visits were too few.[32]

Some women warmed to Christian teachings, including a pleasant friend whose husband divorced her due to her loss of sight. She moved back to her mother's house and it was easy to share the gospel and pray with both mother and daughter. Amina was another who was drawn to the teachings of the Bible. She lived on the island of Moharek and visited the mission house many times, especially during the women's prayer time and always asked when the next one would be. She was easy to love according to Fanny, and was so 'honest and pure.' Another woman came on Mondays and was keen to know about the 'loving, sinless prophet.' She told other Muslim women she 'did not want a dead prophet—he could not help her.' They cursed her and she stopped following Islam, but had not fully embraced Christianity.[33]

Fanny pleaded for prayer for the women of Arabia, 'who have so little to cheer them and who are living in darkness and error.'[34]

Ladies' Meetings

Of the Sunni and Shia branches of Islam, the former is more influential in Bahrain, as the national leader is Sunni. The two groups share core Islamic beliefs but maintain separate mosques, marry within their communities, and differ in some practices such as the manner of washing before prayer and in some funeral rites.[35]

Both Shia and Sunni women conduct ladies' meetings. The Sunni hold perhaps four a year, whereas Shia women gather repeatedly to remember prominent women and men, especially during the Muslim month of Muharram, when they recall the deaths of Hussein and others in Karbala, Iraq in AD 680. They highly esteem Hussein and believe he 'intercedes for them, and all this mourning in memory of him, is like an open gate into paradise.' He is 'a martyr, an intercessor and Saviour.'[36]

One day Fanny passed a Shia women's *matam* or meeting room, where women readers were hired, particularly on religious occasions. It was the month of Muharram, so the *matam* was hosting readings for ten days. As Fanny entered and sat near the door, women crowded around, asking what she wanted, while others wanted her evicted. Some recognised her and ushered her to a place of honour beside a reader.[37]

The crammed room was shrouded in black as a memorial to Hussein.[38] She heard a mention of Jesus, indicating his association with the events at Karbala. She also heard the ladies in response to a reader, pleading aloud to Hussein, 'We have none but thee to help us.' She heard no mention of sin nor how to live in a way that pleased God. Instead, they exalted and wept for a man who was dead.[39]

The eight readers each read for under five minutes, but sounded croaky as it was the seventh day of Muharram. The leader waved a black cloth to signal various responses while the women stood, kept the beat with their feet or pounded their chests from grief. Fanny caught sight of their bruised chests as they worked themselves up with loud sobs and cries. A reader implored Fanny through tears, 'Oh Christian, behold this day!'[40]

Water and coffee were later distributed, along with tobacco pipes constructed from a clay jar and a small holder of charcoal with a bamboo handle. Fanny declined to smoke, which was duly noted and commented on. She estimated 99 percent of Shia ladies smoked them, while no Sunni ladies partook. Fanny mused on the attraction of these regular gatherings. The readings do not vary and the women do not listen, so perhaps it is the 'pipes and coffee and any little bits of gossip' that brought the ladies in.[41]

In stark contrast to the mournful Shia gathering, Fanny attended a Sunni ladies' meeting to celebrate Mohammed's birthday, which is also marked by the Shia. She was struck with the rainbow of new frocks in purple, orange, green, and magenta. Women wore all the jewellery they owned in addition to hanging 'ornaments' and 'jasmine and bunches of sweet smelling greens . . . on the braids of their hair.' She also noted the henna-stained hands. 'Not content with finger rings they dye their hands and decorate them with a yellow and black stain, which they think is very becoming.'[42]

Like the Shia gathering, readers persisted as the women mingled. Fanny could not discern the gist of the readings, but only 'a mass of endless repetitions and jingling rhymes.' The women replied en-masse with 'ya Allah' (O Allah). All the while, coffee was served with pots in the left hand and cups in the right.[43] This regime was obligatory, as the culture dictates that food or drink is served using the right hand.

As she huddled in these gatherings, Fanny sensed Satan's efforts to make her despair. She concluded that yes, 'God is able to raise these dead, dry bones and make them a living army to His praise and glory.'[44]

Day Visit

Fanny was active at the hospital, doing 'all the bandaging on the women's side.' [45] In addition she walked home with women patients to maintain contact and enter new homes.

The missionaries also visited outlying villages. One Wednesday after prayers, Fanny and a colleague loaded donkeys with books and medicine and set out for Budiya, where the school master opened his school for the missionaries to host a clinic. Fanny counted twenty to thirty women who pressed indoors as she unpacked some basic medicines.[46]

Fanny was in stride with the Arabian Mission, whose primary means of mission work was Scripture distribution and medical work.[47] She told the gathered women the medicines were free, but first they wanted to share 'some good words from God's book.' In response, many of the women replied with the Islamic creed, 'There is no God but the one God, and Mohammed is His prophet.' The last phrase did not concern Fanny, as her job was only to speak of the Lord. While the women awaited the medications, Fanny spoke to them about Jesus. The missionaries then pressed ahead with medical work as the women became impatient. The children did not behave like children from Sunday school, Fanny observed.[48]

One patient exhibited bravery when her eyes were examined, yet refused eye drops. So, Fanny administered some into her own eyes. While Fanny measured each woman's pulse, they became amiable and mused why the missionaries rode on donkeys to see them; one even suggesting it was to gain God's favour. The visitors were content for God to reward them 'for being good to the Moslems.' [49]

The missionaries sold six Scripture portions in this village, in contrast to others where women would not even accept a Scripture portion for free. A colporter accompanied Fanny to villages farther away, but she only took a 'donkey-boy' to nearby villages who cared for the animal during visits. Fanny solicited prayer for a good donkey—'if a good one comes along, a four hours' ride is not a hardship.' [50]

Muscat, 1911–1931

Fanny moved to Muscat in present-day Oman in 1911 to oversee the Arabian Mission's women's ministry.[51] She missed familiar scenes in Bahrain, especially as Muscat was surrounded by bare rocky terrain.[52]

Fanny carefully studied the Omanis and believed she would not have been welcomed into the palace if she had not heeded their ways.[53]

Fanny shared a house and meals with mission colleagues and for a time employed a rescued slave boy, who was nearly a Christian.[54] She found the Omani women less fanatical and friendlier than the Bahrainis,[55] crediting her predecessors who had gone before.[56]

Fanny's Arab name was Noorah, which means light, and she was diligent in her work.[57] As she traversed Oman's stony trails to visit villages, she heard children announcing her arrival, wondering why it had taken so long for her to visit.[58] Women's work was Fanny's purview and she was methodical according to Miss G.Y. Holliday, a visitor. Miss Holliday had just been in Bahrain, where many Arab and Persian woman enquired about their 'Lady of Light.'[59]

Visiting was preferable in cooler weather so Fanny could sit indoors with the women away from prying ears on nearby rooftops.[60] She daily sought out women as they sat outside their houses or collected water at a well or food in a field, seeking access to more and more homes.[61] When someone died, Fanny was sure to visit the home of the deceased where neighbours and relatives consoled the bereaved. In doing so, she mingled with women from outlying villages so was welcomed and not feared when she travelled to their locales.[62]

Presenting Scripture was a focus for Fanny's visits. She quoted memorised Bible portions, but seldom distributed printed materials as few could read.[63] While Fanny was warmly received, any message contrary to Islam was repelled.[64] They were hazy on the topic of sin, yet secure as 'the true believers,' wrote Fanny, because 'God looks with special favor on them.'[65] While women trusted Fanny with their secrets, they would not accept the Fatherhood of God nor Jesus His Son. They acknowledged what Christianity did for Fanny and what they were missing. They assured Fanny she was superior to them but they would not accept the Saviour.[66]

Along with Scripture, Fanny always had a supply of medications.[67] Once she visited a sick woman and when Fanny opened her Bible, the woman refused to listen. Fanny noticed a neatly-wrapped Koran nearby, although this lady was illiterate.[68]

Chapel and Sunday School

Sunday mornings saw missionaries and local men and women gather at the Arabian Mission chapel for an Arabic service—an English one was held on Sunday afternoons. One of the missionaries preached and they sang Western hymns translated into Arabic.[69] Without a church bell to summon attendees, Fanny invited people to come. She received amiable replies, even though they did not always attend as promised.[70] Some came who knew of the hospital, as widespread malaria had introduced the mission doctor to many patients.[71]

The chapel sat sixty and was often crowded. It was one of four buildings belonging to the mission on the outskirts of Muscat—two were for accommodations and another was a three-room dispensary,[72] with Bibles being sold in a shop in the market.[73]

Two mornings a week, Fanny taught two children at the Sheikh's palace and always read some Scripture to them. She also taught Sunday school to between fifteen and sixty-five children. Some children were Arabs, but most were Baluchi, an Indian-Iranian people originally from southwest Asia.[74] This variance in attendance was due to the agitation of parents and others at seeing the tally of attendees. One Baluchi father beat his children and demanded they leave 'the house of the infidel and not listen to the heresy,' while intimidating other parents into keeping their children away. However, two Muslim schools sent their children along to the Sunday school after 'fortify[ing] the children with much repetition of the Koran.'[75]

At Christmas it was customary for Christians to distribute small treats, which Fanny gave to her Sunday school children. A week later was New Year's, another event in the Christian calendar. The children returned, looking for more treats, so Fanny asked them for gifts instead. The children later returned, some with 'sticky candy in the palms of their little sweaty hands,' others with walnuts, popcorn, and eggs. Fanny was taken aback and received the gifts with the kindest smile she could muster, then returned them to their donors, substituting the eggs for a coin.[76]

Marash

Some risked a great deal in coming to Fanny to learn about the veracity of Christ. One was Marash, one of Fanny's household helpers who disclosed:

> I am two-faced; one when with you people, and another face when with my people. The gun is loaded and ready for me the day I embrace Christianity and leave Islam. My brother would not delay for a moment to shoot me.[77]

Marash first encountered Christian teaching at Fanny's Sunday school where he was attentive. He gradually stopped going to the mosque and declined to fast during Ramadan. The community pressured him to return to Islam, but he eventually made the break from Islam and was baptised in the chapel, with Muslims watching through the windows.[78]

With regular teaching, Marash's faith deepened and he became known as 'The Christian.' One summer while the missionaries were away, a shop owner asked Marash why he did not announce he was a Muslim. He replied sagely and without fear. A blind man heard and cried for others to come against Marash to stop his blaspheming, while pleading with Marash to seek God's forgiveness for being an infidel.[79] In later years, Marash helped to run the church meetings, along with a colporter. He was unwell for a long while, but content with what God had for him.[80]

When Marash died, his brother insisted on a Muslim funeral. A local Muslim leader refused to participate and the brother failed to convince anyone Marash was a Muslim. Muslims are buried within twenty-four hours of death, and that twenty-four-hour window was closing, so a son of the Sultan intervened and Marash was buried as a Muslim. He had led his illiterate wife to faith as well, who professed Christ at his burial.[81]

Saints' Tombs

The Omani women invited Fanny to their parties and events and genuinely enjoyed her company. On one occasion, Fanny ventured south along the coast to a dilapidated sort of crypt in Sidab called The House of the Vow, as her friend was about to make a vow. Fanny was the only foreigner among the brightly-dressed local women who wore long narrow silk trousers with gold rings on their toes, fingers, and noses and chunky gold jewellery on their ankles and wrists. On top were colourful silk gowns not unlike a 'harem costume.' Fanny felt irrelevant in her simple white dress, wearing her pin from the Woman's Board of the Arabian Mission.[82]

Once inside, the women shed their shoes and sat on mats. The one making a vow, perhaps for fertility or for children who were ill, circled the three saints' tombs and presented her petition, promising to return with sweets or other goods. When she returned to the group, coffee was served while large cooking pots simmered nearby.[83]

The ground in front of the building was stained with animals' blood. While Muslims deny Jesus shed his blood for them, their rituals were always accompanied by bloodshed. She often thanked God she was not a Muslim while feeling heartbroken as the chatter was bereft of any mention of God answering prayer.[84]

Another saint's tomb was housed in a mosque opposite the Muscat mission buildings. Fanny witnessed a woman enter with her year-old son accompanied by a crowd. The child's head was shaved and the hair collected in a cloth, which was tied up, then affixed to a pole by the tomb. Refreshments followed and sweets and rose water were strewn on the grave, as the mother and child circled the tomb three times, exiting backwards. Later, a woman entered the tomb and removed some of the hair, offering it to another woman, likely for an untreatable malady.[85]

On a Musical Note

Musicians of many varieties thrived in Muscat, including a man who played an instrument fashioned from a dried gourd, date palm sticks, and wire. Although Fanny could not detect musicality, he had a loyal following. Others blew into animal horns for hours, sometimes until 4:30 a.m.[86]

When the Sultan heard some Indian musicians in Bombay, he determined to form his own band, conscripting from among his soldiers. They performed recitals twice a week, playing 'Baa Baa Black Sheep' and 'It's a Long Way to Tipperary.'[87]

During the Islamic Feast of Sacrifice, Muslims commemorate Abraham's willingness to sacrifice his son Ishmael by slaughtering an animal, usually a sheep. On the morning of this Feast, the Sultan's band played the old American hymn, 'There Is a Fountain Filled with Blood (Drawn from Immanuel's Veins).' Few understood its true significance except perhaps Fanny, who prayed the day would come when Omanis would recognise the 'fountain that has been opened for sin and uncleanness' to wash away their sins.[88]

Death of the Sultan

Fanny and her teammates functioned in the context of Omani politics. Inland tribes were not loyal to the Sultan of Muscat and had various quarrels with him. For example, they resented efforts to restrict the sale of guns. During a few of these tensions, some Arabian Mission staff were withdrawn from the interior, while others remained in Muscat and Mutrah, including Fanny.[89] The Sultan suppressed uprisings around the country with help from the British, although rebels neared the capital. The conflict lingered for eight years and was later quelled with a treaty, giving the missionaries easier access to the interior.[90]

When the Sultan of Muskat died, the city mourned his loss. Houses of the poor and rich alike were 'filled with shrieking and wailing,' wrote Fanny. Crowds grieved the loss of the 'father of the poor, father of the orphans.' When Fanny visited a drop-in for women mourners in a palace, there was 'no room to sit or stand.'[91]

In the early 1920s, Fanny travelled to Australia for a longer leave. One niece recalls she was different from others of her generation. When Fanny ate Sunday lunch with some family, she thanked God before the meal was served, only for a child to remark this was not usually done. Fanny was characterised as being 'narrow-minded' by some of her relatives, but she did retain her humour.[92]

Amarah, Iraq, 1931–1936

In retirement, Fanny spent some years in Iraq alongside her colleagues, where she would teach girls the Bible, how to sew, and how to take care of a home. In the winter, the missionaries distributed clothes and food to the poor, including dolls made by donors in the US.[94]

Sunday school for seventy children was 'wild and unmanageable' at first. Things did quiet down and the children keenly retold Bible stories they learned and enjoyed memorising verses and singing choruses. Many came regularly and not just for the small gifts, although being from the most impoverished in the city, they treasured cold-weather clothes given at Christmas.[95]

Two older girls demonstrated a heartfelt longing to know Christ as their Saviour, so Fanny taught them privately.[96] Their spiritual growth was a great encouragement to Fanny, who wept with thanks when the girls prayed on their own initiative. On another occasion, after learning about being thankful, Fanny heard one saying she was grateful for the Scripture, for Jesus's teachings, and for sending Fanny and the other missionaries to Amarah.[97]

A fifth of the country's lepers lived in Amarah.[98] The missionaries met with thirteen women from the leper colony for prayer, including one who was nearing death.[99] She told Fanny she wanted to die as her body was useless. Fanny gently chided her, encouraging her that God would use her to glorify Himself, and He did. During times of prayer, this woman was thankful and expressed her longing to learn about salvation. She persistently spoke of the Lord in the leper community, bringing others to a fuller understanding.[100]

Fanny also assisted in the mission clinic, which saw several thousand patients a month. The Thursday clinic was for the poor, who were seen by a doctor for free—eight out of nine of all patients were among this number.[101] Her colleague Miss Dalenburg reported two hundred women came at one time with their children. Keeping order, wrote Miss Dalenburg, required 'a person with grace, patience, fortitude, firmness, a loud voice and a sense of humor. Miss Lutton is just that person.'[102] Fanny arrived at 6 a.m. and was there until the last of the patients 'picked up her crying babies and broken cup or medicine bottle' and departed.[103]

In Conclusion

Fanny's first impressions of the Arab world were bleak. She was one of the first few women missionaries in the early 1900s in the area and even feared being assassinated as she set out clutching a few Arabic phrases. Initially, she hesitated to venture far from the well where she listened to women and attempt to discern their words. From early on, she sought to explain Christian truths.[104]

During her twenty-seven years of 'notable service,'[105] Fanny welcomed many more mission colleagues and facilities. She was grateful to God for her prayer supporters and for numerous Muslim friends. She was also thankful to hear of a husband and wife who had come to salvation in Christ from Islam. Yes, she concluded, it had been worth it to 'live and labor here in this strange land and among its strange people.'[106]

Fanny retired in the US in 1936 and died ten years later at the age of eighty-six following a brief illness. In retirement, she maintained an interest in the work of missions, particularly in the Arabian Peninsula.[107] A colleague said of Fanny upon her death, instead of expressing sorrow, one would only want to follow in her steps.[108]

Endnotes

1. Fanny Lutton, "Reminiscences," *Neglected Arabia* 126. July–September 1923 (Archive Editions, 1988), 15.

2. Rev. T. H. MacKenzie, "The Log of the Barala," *Neglected Arabia* 116. January–March 1921 (Archive Editions, 1988), 10.

3. "The Luttons in Australia—Sarah and Fanny (3rd Great Aunts)," *Lynelle Briggs: Family History*, 27 May 2019. https://familyhistorybriggs.blogspot.com/2019/05/the-luttons-in-australia-sarah-and.html,

4. ibid.

5. Jerry Zdanowski, *Saving Sinners, even Moslems: The Arabian Mission (1889-1973) and Its Intellectual Roots*. (Cambridge Scholars Publishing, 2018), 172–173.

6. "The Luttons in Australia."

7. Mrs. S. M. Zwemer, "The Girls' School at Bahrein," *Neglected Arabia* 45. January–March 1903 (Archive Editions, 1988), 10–12.

8. ibid.

9. Fanny Lutton, "The 'Acorn' School Once Again," *Neglected Arabia* 60. January–March 1903 (Archive Editions, 1988), 9–11.

10. ibid.

11. ibid.

12. ibid.

13. Jennie A. Scardefield, "My First Sunday in Arabia," *Neglected Arabia* 48. October–December 1903 (Archive Editions, 1988), 7–8.

14. *Neglected Arabia* 49 January–March 1904.

15. Rev. F. J. Barry, "Busrah Chronicles," *Neglected Arabia* 50. April–June 1904 (Archive Editions, 1988), 13–15.

16. "The Luttons in Australia."

17. Barry, "Busrah Chronicles."

18. "Annual Report," *Neglected Arabia* 53. January–March 1905 (Archive Editions, 1988), 3–7.

19. Lutton, "Reminiscences."

20. Fanny Lutton, "Work Amongst the Women at Busrah," *Neglected Arabia* 51. July–September 1904 (Archive Editions, 1988), 11–12.

21. Lutton, "Reminiscences."

22. Lutton, "Work Amongst the Women at Busrah."

23. ibid.

24. "Extracts from Mrs. Worrall's Annual Report on Women's Medical Work in Busrah, 1904, In-Patients," *Neglected Arabia* 53. (Archive Editions, 1988), 10–12.

25. Lutton, "Work Amongst the Women at Busrah."

26. ibid.

27. Rev. Alfred DeWitt Mason, D.D. and Rev. Frederick J. Barny, *History of the Arabian Mission* (New York: The Abbott Press, 1926), 129.

28. Fanny Lutton, "Every-Day Life in Bahrein," *Neglected Arabia* 54. April–June 1905 (Archive Editions, 1988), 12–13.

29. Mrs. A. K. Bennett, "In the Shadow of Islam," *Neglected Arabia* 55. July–September 1905 (Archive Editions, 1988), 3–5.

30. Lutton, "Every-Day Life in Bahrein."

31. ibid.

32. Fanny Lutton, "Some of My Arab Friends," *Neglected Arabia* 61. April–June 1907 (Archive Editions, 1988), 16.

33. ibid.

34. Lutton, "Every-Day Life in Bahrein."

35. Fanny Lutton, "Moslem Women's Meetings in Bahrein," *Neglected Arabia* 84. January–March 1913 (Archive Editions, 1988), 14–18.

36. ibid.

37. Fanny Lutton, "Double Number, Incidents and Outcidents," *Neglected Arabia* 58 April–September 1906 (Archive Editions, 1988), 14–16.

38. ibid.

39. Lutton, "Moslem Women's Meetings in Bahrein."

40. Lutton, "Double Number, Incidents and Outcidents."

41. Lutton, "Moslem Women's Meetings in Bahrein."

42. ibid.

43. ibid.

44. Lutton, "Double Number, Incidents and Outcidents."

45. Martha C. Vogel, "First Days at Bahrein," *Neglected Arabia* 57. January–March 1906 (Archive Editions, 1988), 21–22.

46. Fanny Lutton, "Miniature Tours," *Neglected Arabia* 66. July–September 1908 (Archive Editions, 1988), 11–12.

47. Mason and Barny, *History of the Arabian Mission*, 71.

48. Lutton, "Miniature Tours."

49. ibid.

50. ibid.

51. J. E. Moerdyk, "Business Items from the Annual Meeting," *Neglected Arabia* 77. April–June 1911 (Archive Editions, 1988), 14.

52. Fanny Lutton, "Zenana Work," *Neglected Arabia* 107. October–December 1918 (Archive Editions, 1988), 15–16.

53. ibid.

54. MacKenzie, "The Log of the Barala."

55. Fanny Lutton, "A Day's Picnic with Arab Ladies of Muscat," *Neglected Arabia* 78. July–September 1911 (Archive Editions, 1988), 5–6.

56. Lutton, "Zenana Work."

57. "Another Milestone, Muscat," *Neglected Arabia* 137. April–June 1926 (Archive Editions, 1988) 3.

58. Lutton, "Zenana Work."

59. G. Y. Holliday, "Impressions of the Arabian Mission," *Neglected Arabia* 80. January–March 1912 (Archive Editions, 1988), 18–19.

60. Rev. G. D. Van Peursem, "Muscat in Winter," *Neglected Arabia* 105. April –June 1918 (Archive Editions, 1988), 13.

61. Mason and Barny, *History of the Arabian Mission*, 158–9.

62. Lutton, "Zenana Work."

63. ibid.

64. "Annual Report of the Arabian Mission, Evangelistic Work, the Ministry of Preaching," *Neglected Arabia* 152. January–March 1930 (Archive Editions, 1988), 4–5.

65. Lutton, "Zenana Work."

66. Mrs. Louis P. Dame, "Annual Report of the Mission: The King's Business," *Neglected Arabia* 148. January–March 1929 (Archive Editions, 1988), 20.

67. Mrs. Edwin E. Calverley, M.D., "In the Steps of the Great Physician," *Neglected Arabia* 108. January–March 1919 (Archive Editions, 1988), 6.

68. "Annual Report of the Arabian Mission, Evangelistic Work, the Ministry of Preaching."

69. MacKenzie, "The Log of the Barala."

70. Lutton, "Zenana Work."

71. Van Peursem, "Muscat in Winter."

72. MacKenzie, "The Log of the Barala."

73. "Annual Report of the Arabian Mission," *Neglected Arabia* 140. January–March 1926 (Archive Editions, 1988), 3.

74. "Another Milestone, Muscat."

75. Reformed Church in America, *53rd Annual Report of the Woman's Board of Foreign Missions* (76. Fanny Lutton, "A Moving Picture on New Year's Day in Maskat," *Neglected Arabia* 132., January–March 1925 (Archive Editions, 1988), 9–10.

77. "Another Milestone, Muscat."

78. Rev. G. D. Van Peursem, "Faithful Until Death," *Neglected Arabia* 157. April–June 1931 (Archive Editions, 1988), 7–8.

79. "Annual Report of the Arabian Mission, Evangelistic Work, the Ministry of Preaching."

80. "Annual Report of the Arabian Mission, 1929–1930," *Neglected Arabia* 156. January–March 1931 (Archive Editions, 1988), 7.

81. Van Peursem, "Faithful Until Death."

82. Lutton, "A Day's Picnic with Arab Ladies of Muscat."

83. ibid.

84. ibid.

85. Samuel M. Zwemer, *The Influence of Animism on Islam: An Account of Popular Superstitions* (London: Central Board of Missions and Society for Promoting Christian Knowledge, 1920), 66–86. Accessed 12 April 2022. https://www.answering-islam.org/Books/Zwemer/Animism/chapt4.htm.

86. Fanny Lutton, "The Maskat Band," *Neglected Arabia* 110. July–September 1919 (Archive Editions, 1988), 11–12.

87. ibid.

88. ibid.

89. Jas. A. Cantine, "Where We Work," *Neglected Arabia* 84. January–March 1913 (Archive Editions, 1988), 6.

90. "MacKenzie, "The Log of the Barala."

91. Fanny Lutton, "Women's Number, Maskat in Tears," *Neglected Arabia* 89. April–June 1914 (Archive Editions, 1988), 5–8.

92. "The Luttons in Australia."

93. "Personalia," *Neglected Arabia* 156. January–March 1931 (Archive Editions, 1988), 16.

94. "Annual Report of the Arabian Mission 1931, Evangelistic Work, Amarah Station" *Neglected Arabia* 161. April–June 1932 (Archive Editions, 1988), 6.

95. *Neglected Arabia* 168. April–June 1934 (Archive Editions, 1988), 4–6.

96. "Annual Report for the Year 1932" Neglected Arabia 164. January–June 1933 (Archive Editions, 1988), 8.

97. Fanny Lutton, "The New Center for Amarah Women's Work," *Neglected Arabia* 165. July–September 1933 (Archive Editions, 1988), 8–9.

98. William J. Moerdyk, MD, "A Leper Colony," *Neglected Arabia* 166. October–December 1933 (Archive Editions, 1988), 10.

99. "Annual Report of the Arabian Mission for the Year 1933, Amarah."

100. Lutton, "The New Center for Amarah Women's Work."

101. "Annual Report of the Arabian Mission for the Year 1933, Amarah."

102. "Annual Report of the Arabian Mission 1931, Medical Work, Amarah," *Neglected Arabia* 161. April–June 1932 (Archive Editions, 1988), 16.

103. "Annual Report of the Arabian Mission for the Year 1934, Amarah," *Neglected Arabia* 170. January–March 1935 (Archive Editions, 1988), 4.

104. Lutton, "Reminiscences."

105. "Personalia," "*Neglected Arabia* 153.", April–June 1930 (Archive Editions, 1988), 16.

106. "Another Milestone, Muscat."

107. "Personalia," "*Neglected Arabia* 210.", July–December, 1946 (Archive Editions, 1988), 20.

108. Reformed Church in America, *115th Annual Report of the Board of World Missions* (New York: Reformed Church Headquarters, 1947) https://digitalcommons.hope.edu/world_annual_report/92

Sarah Hosmon

Sarah was given a motherless Arab baby girl weighing four pounds with clubbed feet while visiting an Omani village in 1936. The baby had the mark of a brand on her forehead, indicating she had been the reason for her mother's death. At first, Sarah refused to keep her, but the baby's grandfather gave Sarah papers allowing her to keep the baby as her own, so Sarah named the baby Ruth and repaired her feet. Later, a Koranic judge demanded Ruth be returned to her family, so Sarah prayed and wrote to the Sultan. 'She knows no mother but me,' pleaded Sarah. Sarah's petition was granted and Ruth went on to study the Bible in India and become a committed Christian, marry, and have two children of her own.[1]

Sarah's medical mission work with women and children would span fifty years. Many years after her first delivery, she was invited by the sheikh of Sharjah to open a maternity hospital in 1951.[2] She was one of a number of missionary health providers who established facilities in the region in the 1950s and 60s before oil money began to flow. The Sarah Hosmon Hospital (SHH) was the first in the area and operated until 1994.[3] The former hospital became a small museum exhibiting its history, housing some equipment, beds, and explanatory notes from the facility in the former *majlis* or sitting room.[4] Currently, it is a venue for art installations.

Sarah was born on a Kentucky, USA farm in 1883. She was ten years old when her mother died. Two years later, an accident resulted in Sarah losing a leg. At the age of fourteen, during a time when she was particularly missing her mother, the Lord drew Sarah to Himself. 'It was a quiet conversation,' she wrote, 'between the Lord and me.'[5] Her pastor encouraged Sarah in her spiritual growth, spurring her on to attend prayer meetings and to share her faith.[6]

Because of her prosthesis, Sarah could not join in play and sports, so she prayed for her friends. God imparted to her a world vision, directing her thoughts towards Asia.[7] She entered into medical studies and although her father would not help her with finances, she saw the Lord provide.

While at medical school, Sarah heard Samuel Zwemer speak about the need for women doctors in Arabia. Expectant Arab women were barred from seeing a male doctor, resulting in needless suffering and death. In addition, medicine was a vehicle with which to spread the gospel. Dr Zwemer's plea touched Sarah's heart and she resolved to go.[8]

Sarah graduated from the College of Physicians and Surgeons at the University of Illinois, USA in 1910, one of a few women among the new cohort. In 1911, Sarah joined the Arabian Mission, the agency co-founded by Zwemer, and sailed to Bahrain to commence Arabic language studies.[9] Her long sea journey allowed for a gradual change of scenery and cultures.[10]

First impressions

At first Sarah felt 'hopeless' as she sought to navigate Bahrain's slender alleys. She soon appreciated those narrow streets, as their windowless walls blocked the sun. The few women she encountered outdoors were swathed in black, so she was 'pleasantly surprised' to see them face-to-face in their homes. She was 'charmed by their low voices and quiet manners' and 'could not keep from loving them at once.'[11]

Initially Sarah thought the women's indoor dresses were unattractive with their 'loud and contrasting' colours. In time she came to enjoy the vivid hues, a welcome contrast to the black garments worn outside the home.[12]

The lack of music struck Sarah. She did not hear men whistle like in the US, nor did she hear Arab women singing lullabies to their babies. When she heard boys sing in minor keys, she contrasted it with music in heaven, which will be 'in all the major tones.'[13]

As with most language students, Sarah was daunted by Arabic language acquisition. 'It is no little task,' she wrote, 'to learn to converse with the women.'[14]

Muscat

After two years of language study, Sarah passed her exams and moved to Muscat, Oman in 1914 for 'women's medical work.'[15] Her first impression of the town was its 'severely barren, bleak and hilly coast,' causing her to wonder who could live there.[16]

Sarah became the first woman doctor at the Muscat clinic envisioned by James and Elizabeth Cantine,[17] which was now under her purview.[18] During the first three months Sarah treated 202 patients,[19] or 5 to 10 patients a day.[20] This rose to fifty to ninety patients a day twenty years later.[21] In dispensing medicine, Sarah wondered about the feelings of the Omanis when first proffered drugs from this stranger. As they took their first sip, she saw their lips move as they recited Koranic verses for protection.[22]

Initially, she was the sole medical worker and was 'so happy in her work,' she reported, 'that she never thinks of being lonely.'[23] Her only lament was that the women did not arrive on time for their appointments.[24] The work grew and in time, patients gravitated from across Oman to be treated by Sarah, who 'cared for the women of Muscat, body and soul'.[25] Paediatrics became a focus, with increasing numbers of women entrusting their babies to Sarah's care.[26] She was gratified to see 'thin babies grow sturdy and happy,' wrote Sarah, 'under careful feeding and proper treatment.'[27]

In accordance with the conventions of the Arabian Mission,[28] Sarah commenced each clinic with a gospel presentation. The female patients listened, but she found the poor ones received the gospel 'more readily.' For two years she used the same Bible texts in the hope it would be remembered. The content would 'enable every soul to find Christ as his Savior,' she wrote, 'if he will heed the exhortation given.'[29] Her plan was to 'present Jesus Christ as Lord and Savior' without reference to the Koran or to Mohammed. She sought 'very earnestly' to focus on 'the beauty of our Blessed Lord, on His Holiness, His purity, His love and the power of the Blood of Christ to cleanse.'[30]

Sarah met a range of women, including 'secluded women in the royal family, wives of Hindu merchants, and Bedouin women from the desert and seacoast.'[31] Her treatment of a cousin of the Sultan of Muscat led to the missionaries acquiring land for a new hospital.[32] The ruler of Sohar also beckoned Sarah to help his wife. She was there for a month, during which time her Bible presentations were heard by 'Koran teachers, judges, sheikhs, merchants, and Bedouin.'[33]

One day, Sarah received an impressive visitor from a prominent family. The guest was quiet as Sarah showed her some books, her organ, and her typewriter, but eventually began to open up. She was married at eleven-years-old to a relative, who brought her to Muscat from the interior. She cried for a doll to play with and when she tried to escape, her husband whipped her, then married the girl's servant. She was illiterate, had borne three children and been 'kept in rather closely all her life.' She often visited Sarah's dispensary and listened closely to the gospel.[34]

Sarah cherished the position of women presented in the Bible, as being co-heirs with Christ along with men (Rom. 8:17). She contrasted this with the status of women in early twentieth-century Arabia. Her first obstetric case was the delivery of a baby girl. Once the gender was revealed, 'there was an instantaneous and simultaneous hush', she wrote. If it had been a boy, the bearer of the news would have been rewarded by the father.[35]

At that time girls received little education, except to learn to read the Koran at the age of four. A few had additional schooling, but generally girls stayed home to acquire skills in sewing and cooking. Many husbands did not allow their wives to learn to write.[36]

When men married their first wife, Sarah noted, the new bride was content and happy to show off her new home. This lasted until the husband took subsequent wives, which did nothing to 'promote peace and harmony.' While visiting, Sarah heard much talk of marital quarrels and bride prices.[37]

A visitor to the Arabian Mission team in Muscat during the World War I noted the missionaries went about their work with 'courage and cheerfulness.'[38] The medical work did not support itself financially, as the people of Muscat were 'very, very poor,' so half the cost of the treatments was borne by the mission.[39]

Sarah delayed her furlough due to staff shortages. She sailed to the US in 1918[40] and returned to Muscat the following year.[41] During Sarah's absence, Mrs Van Peursem ran the Muscat dispensary—she had previously run the hospital and dispensary in Bahrain.[42]

Tours

Sarah was often noted for her journeys to visit those living by the sea, causing one historian to label her an 'avid tourist.'[43] Her 'love for touring in the villages' along what is known as the Pirate Coast surpassed many who could not leave the 'capital area's defensive cordon.'[44]

For two to three months a year, along with Indian nurses, and seated on a donkey[45], Sarah spread the gospel for 175 miles amongst those without resources to visit the clinic.[46] These tours stalled during conflicts between the Sultan of Muscat and sheikhs in the interior.[47] Eventually, Sarah visited outlying villages by car,[48] which was quicker than by 'boat and camel.'[49]

Sarah's tour to Kiryat was a highlight. She attracted needy villagers as well as a prominent woman who had undertaken an eight-hour camel trip to entreat Sarah to visit her town. After a particular session of Christian teaching in Kiryat, Sarah overheard a woman saying her husband had not wanted to leave because 'he did not want to miss hearing the reading from [Sarah's] book.'[50]

Sarah detailed one trip she took with Nurse Salma when they sailed north from Muscat to Sibe. They beached near some huts edged with date palms and two 4,000-foot mountains. Their host was Beebie Thraia, an acquaintance of Sarah, who was visiting her extensive date gardens and who secured the use of a neighbour's hut as a dispensary.[51]

Early on Sarah performed a trichiasis (removal of an ingrown eyelash) on a Sibe woman named Heela, who shifted away whenever Sarah read the Bible. When Heela returned for a second procedure with blood-soaked dressings, Sarah wondered why. It turned out Heela had been rubbing sand in her eyes instead of water to perform the ritual washings at prayer times, as she had been advised to keep her dressing dry. Blood seeped from her eye as she prostrated for the five daily prayers.[52]

On day two, Sarah was summoned to the home of a wealthy man, where she performed another trichiasis on a woman named Sharifa. As she proceeded, Sharifa's relatives panicked because the patient was so still. 'They would have cried for help,' Sarah wrote, had she 'not succeeded in calming them.' Sharifa was memorable, with her 'quiet sweet way,' her gratitude, and how she listened to the gospels read by Sarah.[53]

Sarah and Salma spent their mornings in the dispensary. Afterwards, they sought out villagers and those in the fishing community, often attracting a crowd. Sarah first read to her patients from John chapter 1, then chapter 3 to explain how the Word 'had come to give us a new life by a new birth.' She followed this with Mark 7:21–22 about the need for this new birth before returning to John chapter 3. Sarah found the Sibe women 'open' and 'friendly,' so much so that they had 'no obstacles in reading to them.'[54]

When Beebie Thraia realised Sarah was taking every opportunity to 'win the women to Christ,' she no longer accompanied them on their forays. Sarah thought their persistence in sharing from the Bible would cool relations with their host, but Beebie Thuraia remained hospitable.[55]

When Beebie Tharia's house was destroyed by fire and ants, she reverted to sleeping in a date hut similar to Sarah and Nurse Salma's humble accommodations. Sarah and Salma sometimes sang Arabic hymns in the evenings and Sarah would visit Beebie Tharia and often read Scripture to her:

> One evening while I was reading the life of Joseph I wished I could have taken her picture as she sat bent over drinking in every word. Joseph's beautiful forgiving spirit was such a contrast to the 'eye for eye, tooth for tooth' spirit among the Moslems. When I had finished it was late and as I was

leaving I said to her, 'You have asked me where is the truth. Now do you see which book tells the truth?'[56]

Sibe women gathered dry wood, carried well water, and pounded coffee. Their slate of duties lent room for Sarah and Beebie Thuraia to speak openly. Beebie Thuraia 'never resisted the gospel', wrote Sarah, but showed 'a questioning after something better than she now experiences.' She had read two gospels and Sarah gave her the entire Bible, from which Sarah heard her reading selected passages.[57]

The morning they departed, Beebie Thuraia walked 'all the way to the water's edge' along with a good number of others who said goodbye, entreating them to return.[58]

On a later tour north of Muscat, Sarah reported an increasing number of Bedouin women who came, some walking for three days to receive attention for a sick baby. A local leader showed interest in the missionaries' work. His soldiers respected the missionaries, some borrowing Sarah's Bible and 'reading it for hours at a time.'[59]

Nurses

Sarah grappled with the retention of nurses. Without a community of local believers to draw on, nurses were recruited from countries outside the Gulf like Syria and India. Barriers to recruitment were myriad, including living in a sea of Islam and Arabic language acquisition for the Indians. In their home countries, there was a great variety of fruit and vegetables, while the diet in the Gulf was unvarying and malaria was unrelenting. On top of all this, relatives wanted them to return, as incomes in their home countries would be higher.[60]

Sarah did engage a number of Indian nurses and found one in particular to be 'willing, faithful, [and] efficient'—Nurse Mary. During

Sarah's furlough in 1932, Mary carried on the women's work, constantly assuring the patients that some day a doctor would come.[61]

Sarah nurtured her staff by regularly studying the Bible with them, followed by 'heart searchings and confessions.' They met nightly to pray for their own work as well as for other countries using the Student Volunteer Movement materials. Support also came from outside Oman. A missionary in India had challenged one of the Indian nurses for mission work and 'always remained faithful' in praying for her and sending greetings.'[62]

New Hospital Building

Sarah's verse for 1931 was, 'The lot is cast into the lap, but the whole disposing thereof is of the Lord' (Prov. 16:33). That year, Sarah anticipated touring along the Batina coast, but was waylaid by the death of Marash, who had embraced Christianity, along with his wife. Following his death, Sarah cared for Marash's widow for over four months. Then, Mr Dykstra, who was to oversee the construction of the women's hospital wing, could not come. So, Sarah launched the project herself of building eight rooms and three verandahs.[63]

Sarah had already gathered the building materials. They would only be stolen while she was away during the summer, so, as spring was optimal for going ahead, she 'appealed unto the Lord for help.' As the work proceeded, she was troubled the project would be financially unviable and concerned that she would be taken advantage of by men who would waste time and sell off the materials. The new hospital wing was completed and Sarah even read the Bible to the workers, finishing all of the gospels and part of the Old Testament.[64]

Towards the end of Sarah's time based in Muscat with the Arabian Mission, she experienced 'the best opportunity' to minister to women. She travelled to Shinas, where she saw fifteen to forty attend her

Friday and Sunday gospel meetings. Her medical work was replete, with mothers attending whom Sarah had treated as children. Yet after twenty-five years, she despaired of the poverty that bound her patients. 'It is a cruel mockery,' she wrote, 'to tell a poor mother her baby needs so many ounces of milk every three or four hours, when she has only about two cents for its purchase.' Sarah was also despondent about the women's lack of education and their 'resistance to the gospel.' She closed her last report with a plea for fruit from the many gospels that had been distributed.[65]

The Next Chapter

While on home leave in 1939, Sarah resigned from the Arabian Mission, due to their 'approval of modernism.'[66] She then joined the Independent Board for Presbyterian Foreign Mission (IBPFM), saying this was when the 'best part of her life work began.'[67] Nurse Mary continued to work at the Arabian Mission hospital in Muscat until the mid 1950s.[68]

When Sarah returned to Oman in 1941, she settled in Saham, northwest of Muscat, but continued to traverse the length of the Trucial States on a donkey.[69] She shared the gospel, gave medical assistance to women and children, and conducted weekly Sunday meetings. During a smallpox epidemic along the Batina coast in 1942, Sarah administered 6,755 vaccinations in less than a week.[70] Two years later, Sarah began to petition the British for permission to open a clinic in Kalba on the northeastern coast of the Musandam Peninsula.[71]

In 1945, nurse Edna Barter joined Sarah, lending help to the lone missionary and worked with her for sixteen years.[72] The two women prayed for 'land and more missionaries.'[73]

Following home leave in 1951, Sarah and Edna were disappointed to learn the local leader in Saham would no longer provide housing or a clinic for them. Two days later, the sheikh of Ajman's wife was quite sick. Sarah was nearby in Sharjah and successfully treated her. The ruler of Sharjah desired Sarah to remain, offering room in one of his palaces.[74]

Sarah Hosmon Hospital

Sharjah was 'one of the most conservative' of the seven emirates or princedoms that make up the present-day UAE.[75] Yet its sheikh invited Sarah and Edna to open a hospital, 'knowing full well they were Christian missionaries.'[76] He was aware of the Bahrain mission hospital's 'good reputation' and so granted permission[77] to 'preach on mission premises.'[78] This was essential to Sarah, as she viewed Scripture as the only source of life. Her 'weapon,' she wrote, was 'the Word of God' and she disparaged the use of the Koran when witnessing to Muslims.[79] The Sarah Hosmon Hospital (SHH), as it was known, was 'the very first hospital to open its doors' in the UAE.[80] Although the hospital changed stewardship, it never lost its licence for open Christian witness.

From SHH, a number of health care workers went elsewhere in the Arab world. Joan Elliot (UK) and Wilhelmina van de Wegg (Netherlands) travelled to Dubai in 1964, then on to SHH where they completed six weeks of training, followed by eighteen months of nursing in Raas al Khaima.[81] In 1967 the then ruler of Fujairah welcomed them, where they set up the Fujairah Maternity Hospital. Expectant mothers travelled to this hospital from as far away as Iran to give birth.[82] Aileen Coleman, featured later in this book, also trained at the SHH in the mid-1950s before going on to co-found a tuberculosis sanatorium in Jordan.[83] As late at the 1980s, midwife Sharon Sasse spent two months at the SHH, during which time her 'fears were overcome' about the work, the culture, and Islam. She knew what to expect should she return, which she did, and was working at SHH as the supervisor of the midwives when it closed.[84]

When Sarah was nearly eighty, she spoke at a Christian conference in Saudi Arabia held on an American oil workers' compound. By this time, she was well known in some circles as the founder of a hospital named after her. She stepped onto the platform and the room went quiet—the appearance of a woman 'raised a few eyebrows.' She was 'bespectacled, earnest-looking, and with severely outmoded dress-sense' and was 'incredibly imposing' despite her limp. In attendance was Amal Boody, a Syrian woman who was exploring her role in missions.[85]

Amal was invited to be the elderly Sarah's assistant, accompanying her to meals and meetings. Amal enquired of her charge about the freedom for Christian witness and sharing the gospel in the Gulf. Sarah's answer was affirmative—midwifery brings you 'much closer' to women.[86] Amal went on to train as a midwife and deliver babies for many decades in Fujairah, present-day UAE. Early on, Amal confessed, 'Sarah Hosmon was right,' as she experienced an openness when sharing the gospel with her patients. Even in the husbands she saw an 'open-mindedness and enthusiasm' for discussion.[87]

Sarah worked at the SHH until just before her death in 1963 at the age of eighty. During her last three years in Sharjah, she mentored nurses and taught Scripture. The SHH was handed over to Middle East Christian Outreach (MECO) in 1982, who ran it until 1994. Gordon Draycott, former administrator at SHH recalled the freedom for witnessing at the hospital. The locals 'were impressed with our service,' he said.[88] The missionaries were not in Sharjah for the money they could earn, and did not turn away those who could not pay, including 'poor expatriate housemaids.'[89]

MECO faithfully ran the SHH in keeping with principles set in place by Sarah. Christian literature was on display and videos of Bible stories were played in the waiting room. 'Anything went' inside the hospital premises, according to Draycott. 'We could easily talk about the Lord Jesus,' he said, 'except... that he is the Son of God.'[90] The staff extended an invitation to pray with each patient and presented patients with a small New Testament, according to former midwife Sharon Sasse. Most local women accepted the gospel, because they knew about 'the contract' for Christian witness, while expatriates declined. So, most families in Sharjah had a copy of the New Testament. Outside of the SHH, Sharon said it was difficult to visit women, but they went anyway, which was appreciated.[91] Being midwives ensured they were viewed as mature, rather than 'inexperienced girls,' thus Sharon and her colleagues were deemed acceptable by the local women.[92]

Some local Muslim religious leaders questioned the right of the SHH staff to share about Christianity, but the missionaries always referenced the sheikh. Other clinics opened up by Christians in the UAE did not enjoy the same privileges. The hospital set up in Fujairah by Minnie Van de Weg and Joan Elliot consisted of two houses, one to live in and one for work. The sheikh told the women, 'if you cause Arabs to convert, you will be taken to prison and your goods confiscated.'[93] Minnie and Joan found other ways to witness, including hosting parties for women who had borne their tenth child where they ate cake, played games, and told Bible stories.[94]

MECO closed the SHH in 1994 because they could not find a woman Christian obstetrician. Sharon opined that because many obstetricians were aborting babies, there were few Christians in the field, contributing to the difficulty of finding personnel. The Sharjah government did not want the hospital to close, Sharon recounts. They said to the SHH staff, 'you are part of our history, you were here before oil came, and we do not want you to leave!' When it closed, 'there was a lot of heartbreak.'[95] In the end, though, transferring patients in labour to larger facilities when complications arose proved to be difficult in thickening traffic.[96]

Following SHH's final record on 17 November 1994 is written, 'The End. God bless all who came through this hospital.'[97]

Endnotes

1. *Biblical Missions*, (Independent Board for Presbyterian Foreign Missions, 2010 or 2011).

2. Brooks Glett, "Mama Zulekha is a reminder of those who birthed the UAE—literally." *The National News*, accessed 22 Dec 2022. thenationalnews.com/opinion/comment/mama-Zulekha -is-a-reminder-of-those -who-birthed-the-use-literally-1.746197.

3. Amanda Engineer, "Untold Lives Blog: Dr Sarah Hosmon and the Missionary Hospital in Sharjah." British Library, 23 June 2022. https://blogs.bl.uk/untoldlives/2022/06/dr-sarah-hosmon-and-the-missionary-hospital-in-sharjah.html

4. Prof. Dr. Sc. Norman Ali Bassam Ali Taher Khalaf, "Sara Hosman Hospital at Sharjah Heritage Days," accessed 22 Dec 2022. https://www.youtube.com/watch?v=xT2tpny_hRk.

5. *Biblical Missions*.

6. ibid.

7. ibid.

8. ibid.

9. James Langton, "How superpower rivalry and fears of a pandemic brought the first doctor to the UAE in 1939." The National News, 21 Aug 2020. https://www.thenationalnews.com/uae/heritage/how-superpower-rivalry-and-fears-of-a-pandemic-brought-the-first-doctor-to-the-uae-in-1939-1.1066500.

10. Sarah Longworth Hosmon, MD, "Arabia Through Green Glasses," *Neglected Arabia* 82. July–September 1912 (Archive Editions, 1988), 14–15.

11. ibid.

12. Hosmon, "Arabia Through Green Glasses."

13. ibid.

14. ibid.

15. *Neglected Arabia* 90. July–September 1914 (Archive Editions, 1988).

16. Sarah Longworth Hosmon, MD, "The Woman Doctor in Oman," *Neglected Arabia* 125. April–June 1923 (Archive Editions, 1988), 14–15.

17. Rev. Alfred DeWitt Mason, D.D. and Rev. Frederick J. Barny, *History of the Arabian Mission* (New York: The Abbott Press, 1926), 159.

18. "Mission News," *Neglected Arabia* 90. July–September 1914 (Archive Editions, 1988), 19.

19. "Report of the Arabian Mission for 1914," *Neglected Arabia* 93, April–June 1915 (Archive Editions, 1988), 13.

20. W. Harold Storm, MD, ed. "Annual Report of the Arabian Mission for 1938," *Neglected Arabia* 185. April–June 1939 (Archive Editions, 1988), 4.

21. "Muscat-Matrah" in the "Annual Report of the Arabian Mission for the Year 1934," *Neglected Arabia* 170. January–March 1935 (Archive Editions, 1988), 14–15.

22. Hosmon, "The Woman Doctor in Oman."

23. "News Items," *Neglected Arabia* 97. April–June 1916 (Archive Editions, 1988), 17.

24. "Report of the Arabian Mission for 1914," *Neglected Arabia* 93. April–June 1915 (Archive Editions, 1988), 13.

25. Dr. C. S. G. Mylrea, "The Arabian Mission and the Centenary, What Our Doctors Have Done and Are Doing, 1895-1931," *Neglected Arabia* 160. January–March 1932 (Archive Editions, 1988), 5–8.

26. "Annual Report of the Arabian Mission: Medical Work, The Ministry of Healing," *Neglected Arabia* 152. January–March 1930 (Archive Editions, 1988), 11.

27. "Annual Report of the Arabian Mission 1929–1930, Medical Work," *Neglected Arabia* 156. January–March 1931 (Archive Editions, 1988), 13.

28. Mylrea, "The Arabian Mission and the Centenary, What Our Doctors Have Done and Are Doing."

29. Hosmon, "The Woman Doctor in Oman."

30. "Annual Report of the Arabian Mission for the Year 1935," *Neglected Arabia* 174. January–March 1936 (Archive Editions, 1988).

31. *Biblical Missions.*

32. "Annual Report of the Arabian Mission 1929–1930, Medical Work."

33. "Annual Report of the Arabian Mission for the Year 1935."

34. Sarah Longworth Hosman, MD, "The Girls and Women of Arabia as I Have Seen Them," *Neglected Arabia* 98. July–September 1916 (Archive Editions, 1988) 3–6.

35. ibid.

36. ibid.

37. ibid.

38. Rev. W. I. Chamberlain, "A Tour of the Persian Gulf," *Neglected Arabia* 100. January–March 1917 (Archive Editions, 1988), 7.

39. Hosmon, "The Woman Doctor in Oman."

40. "Missionary Personalia," *Neglected Arabia* 102. July–September 1917 (Archive Editions, 1988), 24.

41. *Neglected Arabia* 111. October–December 1919 (Archive Editions, 1988).

42. Mrs. Edwin E. Calverley, M.D., "In the Steps of the Great Physcian," *Neglected Arabia* 108. January–March 1919 (Archive Editions, 1988), 4.

43. Lewis R. Scudder, *The Arabian Mission's Story: In Search of Abraham's Other Son* (New York: Wm B. Eerdmans Publishing, 1998), 199.

44. ibid., 296.

45. Andrew Thompson, *Christianity in the UAE* (Dubai: Motivate Publishing, 2011), 79.

46. *Biblical Missions.*

47. Rev. T. H. MacKenzie, "The Log of the Barala," *Neglected Arabia* 116. January–March 1921 (Archive Editions, 1988), 8.

48. "Annual Report of the Arabian Mission: Medical Work, The Ministry of Healing," *Neglected Arabia* 152. January–March 1930 (Archive Editions, 1988), 11.

49. "Personalia," *Neglected Arabia* 160. January–March 1932 (Archive Editions, 1988), 16.

50. Mrs. Louis P. Dame, "Annual Report of the Mission: The King's Business," *Neglected Arabia* 148. January–March 1929 (Archive Editions, 1988), 13–14.

51. Sarah Longworth Hosmon, MD, "In the Date Gardens at Sibe," *Neglected Arabia* 116. January–March 1921 (Archive Editions, 1988), 7–9.

52. ibid.

53. ibid.

54. ibid.

55. ibid.

56. ibid.

57. ibid.

58. ibid.

59. "Muscat-Matrah" in the "Annual Report of the Arabian Mission for the Year 1934," *Neglected Arabia* 170. January–March 1935 (Archive Editions, 1988), 14–15.

60. Sarah Longworth Hosmon, MD, "Our Trained Helpers," *Neglected Arabia* 147. October–December 1928 (Archive Editions, 1988), 10.

61. Ruth Jackson, "Annual Report for the Year 1932: Medical Work, Women's Work," *Neglected Arabia* 164. January–June 1933 (Archive Editions, 1988), 12.

62. Hosmon, "Our Trained Helpers."

63. "Annual Report of the Arabian Mission 1931: Medical Work, Muscat Women's Medical Work," *Neglected Arabia* 161. April–June 1932 (Archive Editions, 1988), 22–23.

64. ibid.

65. W. Harold Storm, MD, ed. "Annual Report of the Arabian Mission for 1938," *Neglected Arabia* 185. April–June 1939 (Archive Editions, 1988), 4.

66. Andrew Thompson, *Christianity in the UAE*, 77.

67. Keith Coleman, "Missionary Statesmen of the Bible Presbyterian Church," *Western Reformed Seminary Journal 11.1*. February 2004, 3–4.

68. Jeanette Boersma, "Nurse Mary of Muscat," *Arabia Calling* (formerly *Neglected Arabia*) 241. Autumn 1955 (Archive Editions, 1988), 11–12.

69. *Christianity in the UAE*, 79.

70. International Board for Presbyterian Foreign Missions, "Timeline." Accessed 22 Dec 2022. https://praysendgo.com/timeline/.

71. Langton, "How superpower rivalry and fears of a pandemic brought the first doctor to the UAE in 1939."

72. Gordon Draycott, email, 29 Nov 2021.

73. *Christianity in the UAE*, 79.

74. *Christianity in the UAE*, 80.

75. *Christianity in the UAE*, 77.

76. *Biblical Missions*.

77. *Christianity in the UAE*, 80.

78. *Biblical Missions*.

79. "Redeeming the Time," Vol 5, No 3. Summer 2013, Independent Board for Presbyterian Foreign Missions, 6.

80. *Christianity in the UAE*, 77.

81. "How superpower rivalry and fears of a pandemic brought the first doctor to the UAE in 1939."

82. The British Museum, "Joan Elliot." Accessed 4 Sept 2023. https://www.britishmuseum.org/collection/term/BIOG206178.

83. Annette Adams, *The Desert Rat* (Lafayette: Huntingdon House Publishers, 2022), 27.

84. Sharon Post, email, 17 March 2022.

85. Marion Osgood, *Call the Desert Midwife* (Chichester: Lighthouse Publishing, 2021), 56.

86. Osgood, *Call the Desert Midwife*, 56.

87. *Call the Desert Midwife*, 73.

88. *Christianity in the UAE*, 77.

89. ibid.

90. *Christianity in the UAE*, 81.

91. ibid.

92. Sharon Post, email, 17 March 2022.

93. *Christianity in the UAE*, 87.

94. *Christianity in the UAE*, 89.

95. *Christianity in the UAE*, 81–82.

96. Sharon Post, email, 17 March 2022.

97. "Sarah Hosmon Hospital Records," Box 5 and Box 6, MECO Archive Deposit, 27 December 2018, Centre for Muslim-Christian Studies, Oxford, UK.

Hazel St John

Before the cake was cut, two gunmen burst in. The student birthday party was in a Druze village during Lebanon's civil war (1975–1990). One of the intruders was very 'fierce and black-bearded.' They aimed to take two sixteen-year-old boys who had been out with militia. When the gunmen tried to exit with the boys, Hazel insisted on going along, as did the hostess. The gunmen did not want the women to go, but Hazel rose to her full six feet and told them there was no way they would not go. Hazel was widely known and the intruders knew they could not object.[1]

The vehicles sped through the war-ravaged area, 'as if in ambulances with guns through [the] roof and windows.' They reached a concealed command post and upon entry, the new arrivals were questioned—it was 'quite civil.' Hazel recognised one of the men in charge as the father of a former student which was helpful. Following a cup of tea and 'polite conversation,' Hazel and her students were returned to the Druze village and reunited with weeping mothers.[2] Her intervention saved the boys' lives.[3]

Hazel St John spent forty-three years in Beirut, from 1938 until she retired back to the UK in 1981. Initially she taught at the Lebanese Evangelical School for Girls, then later at Eastwood College, which she co-founded with Amine Khoury. All this in a 'paradise of a country,' according to her sister Patricia.[4]

Early Life and Education

Hazel was born in 1916 to Harold and Ella St John, British missionaries to Brazil. While Ella was visiting the UK to care for her sick father, she gave birth to Hazel. Mother and baby's journey to Brazil was delayed by World War I, but eventually they sailed on an old troop ship that was 'infested with rats.'[5] .

Hazel spent her early childhood in the jungle along with her newly-arrived baby brother Farnham. Her nickname was Pukita, which means 'little girl' in Portuguese, a name she kept in the family who called her Auntie Puck. Hazel thrived in what Ella called 'The House of 1000 Fleas' and joined other children kneeling in the fields banging on tin cans to chase away locusts.[6] But, while Hazel flourished, Farnham languished. So, in 1919, the young family returned to the UK where Patricia was born, followed by two more boys, Oliver and John. Harold returned to Brazil for an additional two years, then commenced 'a life of constant travel.'[7] Ella and the children settled in Malvern, England with her mother and grandmother.

Hazel was a 'born leader' according to her sister, Patricia. Hazel would sit her younger siblings down and tell them exciting stories then sing her own compositions.[8] Ella read stories to her children about 'poor little orphans who lived in slums and died making speeches.' While Ella wept, her children laughed at their mother, yet Ella prayed nightly for each of them at their bedsides.[9] When Hazel was nine, she heard about the second coming of Jesus and feared being left behind. She recalled Revelation 3:20, 'I stand at the door and knock. If anyone hears my voice and opens the door I will come in.' Hazel 'accepted the Lord's offer' to be in her life.[10]

One day, Ella found herself in a sizeable sitting room among wealthy women who had gathered to hear about missionary work and raise funds. Ella felt out of place as she had no pearls or fine jewels to donate, but she did sense the Lord asking what was precious to her. She thought of her three children—the two youngest were not yet born—then strode to the front of the room to present her treasures. In time, Hazel went to Lebanon, Farnham and his wife Janet to

Morocco for thirty years, and Patricia also to that north African country for twenty-five years.[11]

When Ella learned her husband would be away for an extended time, she moved her brood to a mountain village in Switzerland in 1926 for a year where they could live cheaply. Ella had a Swiss nanny who rented out cottages, so off they went. Hazel and Farnham skied to school on beer barrel sides and Patricia on a sled. Ella did not protect her children from every hazard, viewing risk as part of daily life. She was happy for them to clamber up trees, even if they tumbled down.[12] Hazel's grounding in the French language would benefit her later in Lebanon.[13]

Back in England, these children of Harold, a well-known preacher, were not always models of propriety. An uncle recalled taking Hazel and Farnham to a tea shop, where they tried to surpass their record of eating twenty-one small cakes at one sitting. When their uncle refused to purchase peanuts, they ordered some themselves. He paid, 'for the sake of their poor mother,' while the children just laughed at the ensuing lecture.[14]

When Ella's sister moved to Malvern to teach at nearby Clarendon, a small residential Christian girls' school, she enrolled Hazel and Patricia. Ella became a house parent and she and Harold would remain based at Clarendon for many years. Hazel enjoyed studying languages, particularly French and Latin, as well as English and history.[15] She was loath to leave Clarendon, but followed in her mother's footsteps and went to Westfield College in London in 1934 to study French and Latin. She then trained as a teacher at Homerton Teacher Training College in Cambridge.

Teaching

Hazel presumed she would eventually assist her aunt at Clarendon. But Hazel first sought overseas experience, opting for Lebanon because 'the glory of Lebanon' from Isaiah 35 had early on caught her imagination. She applied to the British Syrian Mission and in 1938, along with other new recruits, sailed to Haifa, where Jews and Palestinians were fighting. She and her colleagues were 'hastily bundled into cars' and driven up to Beirut, but were slowed by a substantial sheep herd led by a shepherd. Hazel viewed the delay as a 'good omen' for what would be more than four decades in Lebanon.[16]

Hazel taught at the British Syrian Training College and its school, later renamed the Lebanese Evangelical School for Girls (LESG). The school was begun by Elizabeth Bowen-Thompson in 1860 in the throes of the Mount Lebanon civil war.[17] It welcomed children from all faiths while maintaining a clear Christian testimony. Mission policy dictated that half of the LESG students were Christian, and the other half Muslim and Druze. This continued until the Lebanese civil war (1975–1990), when this proportion was no longer possible, as the school was in West Beirut, the Muslim sector of the city.

Hazel lived with other foreign teachers and some local staff on site. When she felt sidelined by the older missionaries, as she was new and had little teaching experience, she sought out other new teachers for friendship.[18] Hazel relished her time there and worked hard teaching English, French, history, and Bible. She was pleasantly surprised by how much her students learned. She wrote to her mother, 'My form did seem to know everything he (the inspector) asked and they came out with the most staggeringly correct quotations.'[19] When some of her students underperformed, Hazel told them about a girl who described herself as not good and not bad, but 'just comfy.' One student pondered why not just be comfortable, but Hazel demonstrated there was benefit in wanting more from life.[20]

Hazel's purview was forty girls, whom she accompanied to the school's daily Christian assembly. She then taught her share of lessons, visited families of day students, marked assignments, and prepared lessons. Before the civil war, Hazel also assisted with boarding students, as the LESG welcomed girls from across the Middle East, including some from important Gulf families. Some of these girls came to know Jesus as their Lord and Saviour.[21] Students said Hazel's teaching was lively and caused them to desire to learn more.[22] Her desire was for her students to come to know Christ, which she sought to do by caring for them and seeing they had an excellent education.[23]

The school's religious freedom was not curtailed, except when they were required to teach 'ethics' to their Muslim girls for a brief time instead of the Bible. But even during these lessons, all manner of topics were addressed and teachers were able to bring a biblical perspective. Discussions often led to openings for the teachers to explain the gospel.[24] Following a school assembly where Hazel spoke about the Pharisee and the tax collector in Luke 18, a student responded, asking if Hazel could meet with their friend. Hazel prayed that the Lord would bring these students to Himself.[25]

Much to her surprise, Hazel became the principal of the LESG in 1950, overseeing eight hundred girls from twenty-eight countries. In her new position, she continued to teach some classes and required her teachers to visit the families of their students.[26] If any teachers were absent, Hazel would step in and teach. She was also cognisant of poorer girls, those with special needs, and any who 'needed encouragement.' Hazel was strict, though, and accepted no excuses for cheating.[27]

When only a single student passed government exams one year, Hazel modified the curriculum. Graduation that year was somewhat fraught. This was the annual event where graduating students are handed their diploma as they strode across a stage in front of peers, family, and friends. Parents were stunned when they realised Hazel would not alter grades or even hand a blank paper to failed graduates so their daughter could appear to succeed and 'still wear the white dress.' Hazel sat listening to families for hours and offered to drive them home just to end the meeting. She emerged from these encounters 'somewhat battered,' but kept to her standards and later decided weaker students would not sit exams they were unlikely to pass.[28] Under Hazel's leadership, the LESG went from a school requiring subsidies to one that flourished financially.[29] It grew and added more buildings as well as helped to build a sister school in Tyre.

Hazel's time away from school often meant a simple picnic, particularly with those who needed a friend or some respite.[30] Sometimes this involved sitting beside the Mediterranean coast, accompanied by wading in the sea. Winter picnics called for a drive up to the mountains where snow awaited the visitors.[31] When Hazel went on leave in 1966, her sister, Patricia, came to visit, then they drove back to the UK via Jerusalem, Syria, and Turkey. They visited anywhere mentioned in Acts, except islands, as they followed Paul's journeys through Greece, Italy, and Spain. This was all in the name of research for Patricia's book about Onesimus.[32]

Margaret Judson began to teach at the LESG in 1966. Hazel was in the UK on furlough, and Margaret often heard teachers and students referring to Hazel 'with great affection.' She described Hazel as 'tall' and 'elegant.' 'You must be Miss St John,' Margaret said on their first meeting. 'Please call me Hazel,' was the reply. When Margaret was in the staff room one day, Hazel asked Margaret to go to her office. She went along, wondering what she had done. Once in the principal's office, Hazel offered Margaret some ice cream. 'I could see you working,' said Hazel, 'and thought you deserved a break.'[33]

Hazel was skilled at telling stories. When a scheduled speaker did not show up for a school assembly, Hazel stepped in and told the students that her father and mother met when her father was twelve and her mother was two. She proceeded to talk about 'true love,' as seen in Jesus' death.[34]

Hazel's diaries regularly mention her reading material. She read widely, including biographies of Louis Mountbatten, Golda Meir, and Yasser Arafat. She also read books by Charles Colson, Jackie Pullinger, and Corrie ten Boom. After reading a biography of Billy Graham, Hazel wrote of a longing to be 'more in touch and usable by the Lord.'[35] In 1959 Hazel was awarded Lebanon's Gold Medal by its president. In 1971, she was recognised in Queen Elizabeth II's birthday honours with an MBE (Member of the Order of the British Empire) for her contribution to education in Lebanon.

Work with the Blind

Early on, Hazel took an interest in the blind and integrated some students from the Lebanese Evangelical School for the Blind into her school. The LESG hosted Christmas parties for the blind students, but one year they were short of funds for their annual celebration. Just in time, an American friend of Helen Keller contributed some money and the party proceeded. Helen Keller was blind and deaf and advocated for disability rights as well as writing and lecturing internationally on behalf of the American Foundation for the Blind. She visited the LESG while Hazel was the principal. Hazel's interest in the blind continued into her retirement.[36]

A blind woman named Sit Saada is mentioned in Hazel's diaries, who came from a Lebanese mountain village. Part of Sit Saada's 'bright testimony' included God giving her a purpose in life despite her limitations. Nadim Serhal was a blind student who went on to receive a university education—Hazel gave him a job teaching history.[37] Hazel had a particular concern for the Serhals and when she was gifted with two chickens, she remarked, 'how wonderful, I'll take them to the Serhals.'[38] After his first wife died, Nadim remarried and went on to Christian pastoral ministry in the UAE and Canada.

A Druze boy stood out for Hazel—he arrived at the School for the Blind at the age of fifteen and was enrolled as a student. His blindness was due to a bomb explosion, followed by a time of loss and hardness of heart. When he learned about the Lord Jesus, he believed and accepted the gospel. In time, he was able to say with confidence, 'I can thank God now that I lost my sight; but for that I might never have come to know Christ as the light of the world and the light of my life.'[39]

Refugees

Hazel was concerned that her students not only learn but also reach out to their community, including refugees. She led the way, but her first visit to a refugee camp did not go as planned. As soon as she entered the tent of some refugees carrying a bundle of clothes, she was besieged. Hazel tossed some items onto a bed, and as she exited, everything she was carrying was seized. Miss Khairallah, one of Hazel's more experienced Lebanese companions, grasped the initiative. 'When our Lord distributed to the 5,000,' she declared to the refugees, 'He made them sit down first—so sit down'. Some of the children were then taken to a nearby wood for a Bible story. When the visitors left, many pursued Hazel, including a small boy who caught up with Hazel, telling her he did not like how the people had ambushed her. He requested a copy of the gospel, and was given one. It all ended well.[40]

Not one to be deterred, Hazel sought out the poor. She befriended some, hosting them in her home and speaking to them about the Lord.[41] She ensured her students personally met the less privileged by delivering clothes and hosting parties. Charities that received funds from the school sent speakers to further educate Hazel's students.[42] Hazel linked up with Global Care, a British charity Patricia helped to start. It had projects in many countries and began a programme for child sponsorship in Beirut. When Hazel retired back to the UK, she remained involved with the charity.[43]

Eastwood College

In the early 1970s, Lebanon was experiencing some unrest. So, the decision was made to hand over the leadership of the LESG to an Arab. Hazel passed the baton to Katy Tleel, who became the principal, then wondered what she would do. Around that time, Amine Khoury, a twenty-year-old Lebanese Christian man, informed his father he wanted to open a school in a six-storey building owned by the family. Amine had been educated in a traditional school and wanted to open a school that offered a 'holistic' education.[44] His father said yes, if Amine could find someone to run it. Hazel's mission colleague Joy Jones was helping Amine's mother with her English and heard about Amine's vision. Joy introduced Amine to Hazel.[45]

Providing her mission agency agreed, Hazel would join Amine in this new venture. Her mission was 'hesitant' for a 'well-known educator' to support a school that might be a 'competitor' to their schools. After many meetings, Hazel did join the new venture to transform a block of flats into a school. She was a 'go-getter' according to Amine's brother Edmond.[46] Despite the age difference of almost forty years, Hazel and Amine worked well together.[47]

Hazel wanted to open a school that was a 'happy place' and one that had good educational standards. Most importantly, she desired this school to be a place where children were 'attracted to Jesus Christ.' She admitted this would largely be through the lives of the staff and teachers. Over the years, Hazel later reflected, they witnessed little apparent response to the gospel. In ensuing years, she heard from students who had come to recognise the truth of what they had absorbed and that Christ could meet their needs.[48]

Eastwood College opened in 1973 with ninety-nine students, and today has one thousand students on two campuses. As the first principal, Hazel's 'unique personality' earned admiration from the school community. She had a deep love for the students, but was 'strict in a loving way.' Although she was well-known, she had the heart of a servant. Edmond recalls Hazel picking up rubbish and throwing it in a bin, something he adopted from her.[49]

At Eastwood, Hazel also learned to cook, as she had lived in a boarding school and now had to fend for herself. She enjoyed entertaining, but found it took a lot of time,[50] and she longed for more confidence as a cook.[51] Nevertheless, she invited many to tea or for a meal and one day a dinner of tabouli (Lebanese salad) in the kitchen with three friends saved her from feeling 'rather homesick and lonely.'[52] She itemised her menus in her diary and included comments like, 'must learn how to do that better' and 'rather successful really.'[53]

Wars and Cars

Cars were one aspect of her life where Hazel acknowledged that men knew better. While navigating Beirut's notorious traffic and dodging bullets, she was dismayed when her car would sometimes stop working. On one occasion, the car battery fell out through a hole in the car's floor and another time the car would not work as it had no fuel. When she was rescued, she wrote in her diary, 'Of course, it started perfectly for a man!!'[54] When Amine's father had Hazel's car fixed and Amine's brother Edmond paid for it, Hazel could only exclaim, 'Aren't men wonderful?'[55]

When times of unrest and war came, starting in 1939 with World War II and continuing through the 70s with the start of the Lebanese civil war that lasted decades, it was challenging for Hazel to proceed as she could when there were times of peace. The commencement of World War II delayed Hazel's return to Beirut following a home visit. She did manage to find transport in January 1940, but life was different in Lebanon with soldiers stationed there. In 1943, Hazel was evacuated to Jerusalem for six months by the British Embassy along with other women and children.[56] She found it hard to be apart from her students, and as returning was difficult, she counted up other job offers, including one from her aunt to take over as head mistress of Clarendon. Hazel was relieved someone else took up that position,[57] although the following year, she left Lebanon and taught at Clarendon from 1944 to 1948.[58]

During the course of World War II, Hazel and her colleagues welcomed soldiers from Britain, Australia, and New Zealand for tea and English conversation, and witnessed a tremendous response to Bible studies. One Canadian soldier named Harry was particularly memorable. When his submarine was hit by a torpedo, he was trapped. Harry recalled what his Sunday School teacher had written on the board: 'Believe on the Lord Jesus Christ and you will be saved.' Harry cried, 'I believe!' and was then inexplicably ejected through a hatch and taken to safety. He was still shaken by the event the next day when he heard some singing while walking in Beirut. He found his way to Hazel's and became a fast friend, telling anyone and everyone of God's love for him.[59]

The Lebanese civil war broke out in 1975, two years after Hazel transferred to Eastwood College. Hazel was asked by the British Embassy in Beirut to be a warden for 98 British citizens in eight villages. During one meeting, wardens were encouraged to stay but make contingency plans. Within 10 days, the wardens were told to phone those on their lists and suggest people consider leaving Lebanon. On one visit to the British Embassy, Hazel saw it was besieged by Lebanese in search of visas to the UK.[60]

Eastwood College was home for Hazel and during one volley of bullets, she cowered with her maid who managed to go to the kitchen, just as a bullet hit the chair where she had been sitting. On another occasion, due to accelerated fighting, Hazel was evacuated in a tank.[61] She moved frequently and was often an overnight visitor in the home of David and Margaret Judson, especially when it was too risky to stay at the school.

Hazel's friends were so important that she would drive through dangerous areas to meet up with them.[62] She also highly valued her personal correspondence with friends and family, but there was no regular postal service during the war. So, one weekend, she entered the Beirut airport and found a British man who agreed to take a pile of letters and post them from the UK. Hazel also found a former student who could take letters to her mission leaders in Cyprus.[63]

As the civil war raged, classes at Eastwood continued in fits and starts. In one school year, Eastwood conducted five and a half weeks of classes. During a student debate on the merits of living in Lebanon or Australia, the latter won, but Hazel preferred Lebanon despite all that was happening.[64] With fewer students due to the civil war, teachers' salaries were difficult to pay.[65]

Hazel's diaries were replete with daily prayers for deliverance but mostly with thanks. Daily she placed her concerns before the Lord. Would she have enough teachers? Would they have enough pupils in order to pay those teachers? Even lost glasses and an eye infection were lifted to the Lord in prayer.[66]

In 1976, opinions varied widely in her mission team when possible mandatory evacuation was being discussed. Hazel was disappointed to learn they would be compelled to fly to Cyprus in April, but was open to attending a conference. She was later pleased to learn she and her colleagues could choose to return to Lebanon in two weeks, although the news was not encouraging, with over three hundred killed in one day.[67] Hazel's mission leader questioned what she would do if she returned.[68]

In nearby Cyprus during her evacuation, Hazel hitchhiked to some mountains, then hired a donkey for an excursion. She regularly schemed to return to Beirut, but no planes were flying as the Beirut airport was closed. While some of Hazel's colleagues remained in Cyprus and established a literature distribution, Hazel did return in early May, but teaching was curtailed, as rockets hit Eastwood.[69] When classes did resume, Hazel enrolled two of the Judsons' children. They loved their English lessons from Auntie Hazel.[70]

On a particularly difficult day during the civil war, an Eastwood school bus arrived with most of the children on board crying. A soldier from Yemen had shot at the bus twice and one of the bullets had penetrated the lung of three-year-old Lara. Both Amine and Hazel spent hours at the hospital, which was appreciated by the family. Thankfully, the little girl recovered.[71]

Georgette, Hazel's former student, lived with her family in a Christian village. One night, some Muslims entered the village, burned homes and massacred anyone they found. Georgette and her family cowered in the basement, listening to people being killed above. In the morning, they re-emerged to find their home had been razed. They had nothing but the clothes they were wearing. Georgette's fourteen-year-old daughter told Hazel about that night. 'Everyone was panic stricken,' she said, but 'my mother was calm and kept praying for us all. I want that kind of faith too.'[72]

One evening, Hazel was driving home, but had forgotten to take the prescribed night time route. Syrian soldiers shot at her car and one bullet entered the vehicle and another hit the rear of the car. She stopped and was soon surrounded by ten soldiers, one of whom got into her car. She backed up to the checkpoint, where the captain was 'very nice, and we laughed.'[73] When two missionaries married at All Saints Anglican Church near the Mediterranean during a brief lull in the fighting, the streets were eerily quiet. En-route to the reception at Eastwood, David and Margaret Judson paused to allow some masked gunmen to cross in front of them and take cover. Hazel caught up with them, oblivious to the ensuing dangers and called out, 'I do like driving on empty roads!'[74]

In October 1978, Hazel fell in the street and knew she had broken her left leg. There was no one around until two 'charming and scruffy' fifteen-year-olds came upon her, offering to help. They asked for her car keys and much to Hazel's relief, returned with her vehicle. She managed to ease herself into the back seat and the two boys drove her to the home of some friends, who transported her to the hospital.[75] The next day, she felt weepy, but managed to pull herself together with help from the Lord. As she recuperated, she received dozens of visitors, including a surprise visit from her sister.[76]

Hazel's crutches proved helpful. One day she inadvertently drove past a Syrian checkpoint without stopping. As the irate soldier prepared to shoot, Hazel's passengers cried out, and she backed up her car and apologised profusely. 'O Monsieur, I'm SO sorry,' she said. 'You see, I broke my leg and these are my crutches,' which were protruding from the window. The baffled soldier waved them on.[77]

Hazel, Faith Willard, and Heather Rogers lived together at Eastwood. At Faith's initiative, they fasted on Friday, then spent their Saturdays offering Bibles, tracts, and other Christian material to Syrian soldiers who were stationed in Lebanon. The women reasoned that Lebanon had religious freedom, and missionaries had all been expelled from Syria. Besides, most of the Lebanese despised the Syrian soldiers, so off the women went, sometimes accompanied by Brenda de Smidt.

One Saturday, Hazel and her friends gave out forty-eight New Testaments and Billy Graham's book *Peace with God* in five Syrian camps. At every camp, they asked for the leading officer, who took books for each of their men. Hazel prayed, 'Please Lord, use and bless these [materials].'[78] Another time, they were 'thrilled' to give forty-six New Testaments to some soldiers from Saudi Arabia.[79] On a subsequent outing, Hazel and Heather were later arrested, as the commanding officer thought they were distributing Jewish propaganda.[80] At one camp, Hazel was questioned by a Syrian general for some hours. Hazel explained the gospel to him and he told Hazel he did not want just a New Testament, but the entire Bible. The women later learned this general was one of the most important Syrian military leaders in Lebanon at the time.[81]

One memorable Saturday, Hazel, Faith, and Brenda spread out their picnic and a map of the area, and soon two soldiers stopped to make enquiries. The women drove on and gave out 140 New Testaments in a few villages. Then, two other soldiers pursued them and one got in the back seat of the women's car and directed them to go to their leader[82] while his gun rested on Faith's head.[83] Their new passenger spoke to the women in English and was 'very affable.' At the camp, they were questioned by soldiers, who assumed the women were spies, while Hazel kept offering Bibles to officials.[84] They stayed at the camp for an hour and were served fruit and coffee. The captain was happy to receive a New Testament as well as one for each of his men, although an officer waiting outside made his men return the gifts. On the way home the women were 'shot at once from a checkpoint they missed' stopping at but concluded they had had a great day. They were home by 6 p.m. and made potato salad for church the next day.[85]

When Faith wanted to photograph war-damaged buildings, Hazel cautioned against it. Faith did scan the area, then photographed a building heavily pock-marked with holes from shells. She quickly got back into the car, but a Syrian soldier approached their vehicle asking for Faith's camera. Hazel released 'a barrage of chatter,' saying one of her students lived in this particular building. 'On and on she went,' then finished by offering sweets to the soldier, who waved the women away.[86]

Hazel enjoyed the outdoors and Lebanon's beauty and would invariably ask her companions if it would be 'terribly worldly to pick some flowers?' Around lunch, Hazel asked if it was 'worldly if we stopped for lunch?' Sometimes, Faith and Heather delayed lunch until she asked.[87]

Family

During her years abroad, Hazel would remain close with her extended family, if only by letter and prayer. In Lebanon, the members of her mission became family, and later, Eastwood students. Hazel's family widened with the years but she did not discard one part of her family for another as she melded with the ones around her.[88]

Despite many friends and a beloved family, she did feel lonely and on occasion it was 'quite hard.' A diary entry betrayed her feelings of being sidelined and left out, accompanied by mounting domestic responsibilities. The 'time to be happy,' she wrote, 'is NOW,' accompanied by prayer to 'live resolutely.'[89] Another time, she questioned her ability to teach, following a 'tiring day with classes rather noisy.' She was pressed by the need for teachers and Christmas activities. A friend noticed she was looking down and invited her for dinner.[90]

As with most single women in the Arab world, her singleness was questioned. She mentioned a Syrian soldier who wanted to know why she was not married—at this point, Hazel was sixty-one.[91] Hazel did express her joy as a single woman. 'No regrets,' she wrote in her diary,[92] although intriguingly, she did mention meeting a man who had proposed marriage to her 'long ago.'[93]

Hazel could never envision being with the same man all her adult life, but thought men were helpful for carrying luggage and for being partners at cocktail parties.[94] While she did not express a desire for marriage, Hazel was supportive of those who did. She prayed particularly for a colleague, 'Satisfy her with yourself, or if you can send her [a man].'[95]

Retirement

At the age of sixty-five in 1981, Hazel retired from Eastwood College and returned to England. While Hazel loved being in Lebanon, she was 'very glad' she went back to the UK.[96]

Hazel moved in with Patricia, who also never married, in Coventry. Hazel esteemed her published sister and sought to support her work by answering the phone and keeping house while Patricia wrote upstairs. Their days were replete with visiting and receiving friends, delivering meals, attending their church and seeking ways to spread the gospel. When out for a pub lunch, Hazel's waitress was 'ready to listen,' as she had recently lost her seven-month-old baby, and accepted a Gospel of John.[97] The sisters ministered to young men in their Coventry neighbourhood by setting up a pool table in their garage and inviting young people to come and play. Newcomers easily found the house, as local youth directed them to the home of the 'two rather genteel' women 'who had befriended them.'[98]

Ministry Further Afield

Faith Willard arranged for some Eastwood students to attend a Christian camp in the northeastern US in 1980. This led to Faith inviting Hazel and Patricia to help at this same camp for seven summers. Besides helping as devotional speakers, the two sisters were the first to raise their hands to clean toilets, work in the kitchen, or 'any of the most menial tasks.'[99]

Faith invited Hazel to visit Bangladesh for a month to help at a Christian orphanage. By then, Hazel was in her eighties and Faith wondered how she would cope, but Hazel thrived. On an outing, the smallest children from the orphanage were stuffed into a van, with the driver promising to return to shuttle the others four miles to the designated site. Everyone was delivered except Faith and Hazel, who ended up walking the whole way. Faith wanted to chastise the driver, but Hazel suggested they instead assume the driver did as Faith had wished, so he would not be embarrassed. Hazel made four month-long visits to the Bangladesh orphanage.[100]

Hazel also returned to Lebanon several times. During a visit in 1998, she spoke at an Eastwood school assembly, where Amine was eager for her to tell of Eastwood's beginnings. Hazel also attended a LESG reunion of the class of 1959 and another with seventy-two students from Hazel's earliest days in Beirut. Hazel remembered faces, but not names.[101]

Patricia's death in 1993 was particularly hard for Hazel, but she continued to visit elderly friends, receive visitors from around the world, and take in student lodgers from China, the Czech Republic, and Iran. She also spent ten months in Kazakhstan to assist her nephew and his family, putting her in the running for the world's oldest au-pair.[102]

In a speech at Monkton Combe School near Bath in England, Hazel summarised her life this way:

> I've been fortunate in having a full and interesting life and I've met some exciting people, mostly a long time ago. I once had lunch with the emperor of Ethiopia, I've curtsied to the Queen at Buckingham Palace and visited one of the emirs in Kuwait. At the British Embassy in Beirut, [I shook] hands with the kings of Iraq and Jordan before they were murdered, with the kings of Iran and Egypt before they fled their countries. None of them, except perhaps the two whose children I taught, would have noticed me at all.
>
> Yet every morning, I have the priceless privilege of going into the presence of the King of Kings, the Lord of glory and the Creator of the universe, who actually invites me to call Him Father, who loves me and cares about every detail of my life.[103]

Hazel's last overseas trip was to see another nephew in New Zealand. Upon her return, her health quickly declined. As she lay dying, she read 2 Corinthians 1:8 – 'We are confident and would prefer to be away from the body and at home with the Lord.' Hazel died in 2003 at the age of eighty-seven.[104]

Endnotes

1. Faith Willard, speech, no date.

2. Hazel St John, diary, 16 June 1978.

3. Brenda deSmidt, author interview, 18 August 2022.

4. Patricia St John, *Patricia St John Tells Her Own Story* (Carlisle: OM Publishing, 1995), 207.

5. Hazel St John, "The Hazel St John Story," *Keeping in Touch: A bimonthly newsletter of Canley Evangelical Church, Coventry*, Issue 10 (June 2002), 4.

6. ibid.

7. Patricia St John, *Patricia St John Tells Her Own Story*, 9.

8. ibid, 11–12.

9. ibid, 17–18.

10. Hazel St John, "The Hazel St John Story," 4.

11. *Patricia St John Tells Her own Story*, 54.

12. ibid. 25.

13. Brenda de Smidt and Dr Janet St John, *Hazel St John: Memories of a Remarkable Woman Who Became a Legend in Lebanon* (Coventry: Global Care Publishing, 2005), 8.

14. de Smidt and St John, *Hazel St John*, 7.

15. ibid., 8.

16. "The Hazel St John Story," 5.

17. Jean Said Makdisi, Elizabeth Bowen-Thompson, and the Teacher Training College, "Archeology and History in Lebanon," Issue 22 (Autumn 2005), 84–89.

18. *Hazel St John*, 9.

19. ibid., 11.

20. ibid.

21. Margaret Judson, email, 9 May 2022.

22. *Hazel St John*, 12.

23. Judson, email, 9 May 2022.

24. ibid.

25. St John, diary, 16 Jan 1979.

26. *Hazel St John*, 24.

27. Judson, email, 21 April 2022.

28. *Hazel St John*, 12.

29. John Woods, *His Presence Could Not Be Hidden: Proclaiming Jesus in the Middle East, Middle East Christian Outreach, 1860–2006* (Stanhope Gardens: Eider Books, 2020), 155.

30. Judson, email, 21 April 2022.

31. *Hazel St John*, 20–21.

32. Hazel St John, "The Hazel St John Story (continued)," *Keeping in Touch: A bimonthly newsletter of Canley Evangelical Church, Coventry*, Issue 11 (August 2002), 5.

33. Judson, email, 21 April 2022.

34. ibid.

35. St John, diary, 30 December 1978.

36. *Hazel St John*, 15.

37. ibid.

38. Judson, email, 21 April 2022.

39. Woods, *His Presence Could Not Be Hidden,* 155–156.

40. *Hazel St John*, 16.

41. ibid., 17.

42. ibid., 16.

43. ibid., 28.

44. https://www.eastwoodcollege.com/history

45. Edmond Khoury, email, 5 April 2022.

46. ibid.

47. Hazel St John, "The Hazel St John Story (continued)," 5.

48. St John, diary, summer 1986.

49. Khoury, email.

50. St John, diary, 27 February 1978.

51. St John, diary, 29 November 1975.

52. St John, diary, 28 March 1978.

53. *Hazel St John*, 25.

54. ibid., 14.

55. St John, diary, 10 July 1981.

56. *Hazel St John*, 4.

57. ibid., 10.

58. *Patricia St John Tells Her own Story*, 56.

59. *Hazel St John*, 19–20.

60. St John, diary, 30 October 1975.

61. *Hazel St John*, 17.

62. Judson, email, 21 April 2022.

63. St John, diary, 2 April 1976.

64. St John, diary, 7 November 1975.

65. St John, diary, 4 December 1975.

66. *Hazel St John*, 26.

67. St John, diary, 22 April 1976.

68. St John, diary, 23 April 1976.

69. St John, diary, 13 May 1976.

70. Judson, email, 21 April 2022.
71. St John, diary, 5 December 1977.
72. St John, speech, no date.
73. St John, diary, 6 January 1978.
74. Judson, email, 21 April 2022.
75. St John, diary, 15 October 1978.
76. St John, diary, 17 November 1978.
77. *Hazel St John*, 18.
78. St John, diary, 12 February 1979.
79. St John, diary, 3 March 1979.
80. St John, diary, 20 October 1980.
81. Heather (Rogers) Cowan, author interview, 17 August 2022.
82. St John, diary, 17 March 1979.
83. Faith Willard, speech, no date.
84. Brenda de Smidt, author interview, 18 August 2022.
85. St John, diary, 17 March 1979.
86. Faith Willard, speech, no date.
87. ibid.
88. Brenda de Smidt, correspondence with Janet St John, 13 July 2003.
89. St John, diary, 9 June 1978.
90. St John, diary, 16 November 1977.
91. St John, diary, 15 July 1977.
92. St John, diary, 9 May 1980.
93. St John, diary, 28 August 1980.
94. Brenda de Smidt, correspondence, 19 August 2022.
95. St John, diary, 4 February 1978.
96. St John, diary, 30 October 1982.
97. St John, diary, 15 March 1986.
98. Judson, email, 21 April 2022.
99. Faith Willard, speech, no date.
100. ibid.
101. St John, diary, 28–29 October 1998.
102. St John, speech, Clarendon School, no date.
103. St John, speech, Moncton Combes School, no date.
104. *Hazel St John*, 32.

Ada and Ida Stoltzfus

When the Israeli soldiers approached the school compound, Ada Stoltzfus met them at the gate. It was 1967 and Israel was taking control of the West Bank. This included Hebron where Ada and her twin sister Ida were running a boarding school for Arab boys.

> 'As I stood inside the iron grill and faced fifty uniformed soldiers, tough and rough looking in battle garb with rifles held ready to swing into action, I heard a whimper of fear from one of the boys behind me. . . .
>
> The soldiers . . . demanded the keys to our cars. I refused to hand them over.[1]

How did Ada and Ida Stoltzfus come to be in Hebron at such a time? Ada wrote later, 'If we had known the many situations and decisions we would face, we might not have been brave enough. . . . [B]ut . . . God was with us every step of the way.'[2] They sometimes wondered if they were foolish for staying while others fled, according to Ida, but they were there in the name of Jesus.[3]

Beginnings

Ada and Ida were born in 1910 into a Mennonite family in Pennsylvania, USA. After receiving training in teaching and practical nursing, they worked as teachers for ten years. During World War II, their family sent packages to refugees in Europe via the Mennonite Central Committee (MCC), an international Christian relief charity. The twins joined this effort yet longed to be personally involved in helping the poor. So, in 1947, they joined the MCC and set sail for Indonesia, stopping en-route in Calcutta, India. Three days after they arrived in August 1947, India achieved independence from Britain.[4] Waves of people were on the move—Muslims migrated toward newly-created Pakistan and Hindus to India. Due to unrest in Indonesia, Ada and Ida were reassigned to India, where they helped to distribute MCC relief supplies.[5]

Palestine

Following their three-year term, they returned to the US. While Ida was working at the MCC headquarters, she learned about Palestinian refugees. Ada wrote, 'The Holy Land was torn apart, divided, and parceled out in a bewildering way which left many Arabs homeless.'[6] In 1952, the twins set sail for Palestine for a five-year term with a strong sense of calling and duty. They were well underpinned, with committed churches, supporters, and family behind them. The twins were also acquainted with hardship and sacrifice in a way foreign to many, due in part to their farming background. This is according to Gregg Doolittle, former volunteer and current head of the Hebron school founded by Ada and Ida.[7]

Ada and Ida settled in a troubled land. In 1947, the UN proposed partitioning the land between the Jews and Arabs and then war ensued.

Hebron

Hebron is the burial place of Abraham and so is revered by Christianity, Islam, and Judaism. Because of the sisters' proximity to such a significant site, many Christian tour groups stopped by to say hello to the twins when they visited the tomb of Abraham. Aileen Coleman, who was nursing at the Baraka Sanatorium in nearby Arroub, would visit often. She shared meals with the twins and was always delighted with the menu.[8] The twins' relief work focused on helping Arab refugees in the border villages around Hebron.[9] Impoverished farmers fed their families by eating the grain that would have been used for sowing, so they had no crops. They sold their animals and even the wool from their mattresses.[10] Tuberculosis ravaged many, who were reduced to hunger and utter need.[11]

Ada and Ida worked with local authorities, who would help to supply them with the names of children who needed help.[12] The governor and the mayor of Hebron warned the twins to be careful. Anyone who thought Ada and Ida were trying to influence the religion or politics of the people would be hostile. In time, the mayor was the first to welcome them when they moved to his city and would later become a friend to the twins.[13]

Few Christians lived in Hebron, which Ida thought was the most severe Islamic community she had experienced.[14] Yet the twins remained committed to establishing Hebron's sole Christian institution.[15]

Ada and Ida's first assignment was to help refugees in the Hebron area, but the twins were also to create their own jobs. They did this by analysing and seeking the way to deliver aid. They began with Arabic language studies, lamenting the Tower of Babel where God confused languages. During an Arabic church service in Bethlehem, Ada only recognised two words.[16]

The twins learned to drive on the windy roads from the MCC base in Jericho up to Bethlehem and Jerusalem. The first journey was treacherous, as they left the car in a low gear to navigate the narrow way, hoping they would not meet a bus. They were pleased when they arrived, especially when they heard that even the women who worked at the Arroub Sanatorium, where their friend Aileen worked, did not even drive on those routes.[17]

They educated themselves about the work of the MCC and the United Nations Relief and Works Agency (UNRWA) in the area, as well as other relief agencies. At one refugee camp, sewing classes were operated by the MCC. Helpers cut pieces from fabric, which the refugee women sewed together into garments. Once a woman had made a set of baby clothes, another took her place in the class.[18]

Besides the MCC and UNRWA, the twins worked with the International Christian Committee (ICC) to distribute seed, flour, dried egg powder, powdered milk, cooking fat, and cans of meat. They also distributed bundles made at the MCC warehouse in Jericho from donated items. The first distribution was to seventeen tuberculosis patients, each with 'two pieces of clothing, a can of chicken, a bar of soap, and a towel.' Some recipients were too ill to retrieve their package, so they sent a family member, who signed with a thumbprint, as many, if not all, were illiterate. The twins remained in contact with some of these initial TB patients for many years.[19]

Ada and Ida were pleased with their first distribution, but felt inadequate and longed to do more. They wondered if they could perhaps give out some medicines and longed to be trained in caring for TB patients.[20]

The twins were thoughtful in what they distributed. Bundles for families in border villages included clothing, wrapped in a 'coat, comforter, or blanket.'[21] They gave a shirt, trousers, soap, and a towel each to twenty-five boys in Hebron who had 'gone through the court system.'[22] When Ada and Ida received a shipment of dry eggs, they devised a recipe for a type of omelette using garlic.[23]

Driving between Jericho and Hebron took time, so in the name of efficiency, the twins began to look for accommodation in Hebron. They found a bare home with no electricity, then acquired the necessities, including some burners for cooking and for lighting. They found a small stove for huddling around on cold nights, in which they burned olive tree knots, while the rest of the wood was carved into souvenirs.[24] They were the only foreigners in Hebron and two of a few Christians.

Some challenges awaited Ada and Ida in their new premises. When someone tried to break into the unlocked garage, their landlord suggested the twins hire his brother as a guard. They also learned their interpreter was adding a gratuity for himself to the price of wheat the twins purchased for farmers, so they fired him.[25]

Ada and Ida were pleased to be welcomed by local women and invited to eat at the homes of Hebron families. Their days were filled with visits to villages and sewing projects, so they hired local men and women to cook and clean for them, but who also proved to be helpful in other ways. When the twins visited a local sheikh for a generous meal of lamb, rice, and chicken, the twins reciprocated by inviting the sheikh and his family for coffee and sweets. When two sheikhs, their wives, and others arrived carrying four chickens, it was clear to the twins' servant Issa they had arrived for a meal. The twins were expected in Jericho before dark, and besides, they did not have the facilities to cook such a large meal. Issa knew a place that sold prepared meals, so he and Ida left, purchased the food and returned with large trays of steaming chicken and rice. Ida parked near the house and the food was carried in by the back door and all was well.[26] Issa became a trusted friend and advisor and the twins depended on his mastery of traditions and business practices.[27]

A year later, the twins felt they were fitting in well when they served a whole lamb to their guests, prepared by Issa. Ida confessed she began to eat with a fork and knife, then abandoned her utensils and dug in with her hands.[28]

Ada and Ida were short on things to read until some magazine subscriptions arrived and some family members sent them a radio. When newspapers came from home, the twins read every word, including the ads.[29]

Sewing Classes

An existing needlework operation in Bethlehem was soon taken over by Ida and Ada. The local women were eager to earn some money, so the twins set to work. They found a venue and soon had fifteen women in Bethlehem and twenty in Hebron sewing, using fabric woven in Ramallah. The finished products were sold to tourists. Friends in the US offered to make funds available to pay the women for their work immediately, instead of waiting until it was sold.[30]

One woman with six children joined the sewing project. She had come from a wealthy family and as a refugee, she sold part of her UN rations to pay rent while hoping for a return to prosperity. One day she was too ill to present her completed work to the twins and sent her barefoot daughter. The girl asked Ida if she had any extra shoes she did not want, so the twins went through their closet and found some sandals and thick socks. They visited the family in a single room with thin mats for sleeping and not enough blankets to cover them during nights cold enough for snow. The twins came to know the family well over the years.[31]

Ada and Ida hired a local woman named Sitt Azeezah to help with the needlework projects. She cut cloth, interpreted, and helped to calculate payments. Her life savings were inaccessible in a bank on the Israeli side of the border, so she earned money by sitting with a disabled person at night.[32]

Milk and Food Distribution

With help from the UN, the twins opened centres for distributing milk. By 1953, they were serving milk to 2,000 children aged one to fifteen-years-old at three venues. Cross checks were necessary, like when a newlywed man claimed he had five children.[33] Others listed additional names, but it was hard to be critical in light of such need.[34]

The twins' first big project was in the town of Dhahiriya, south of Hebron:

> We had to arrange for the food, beg ICC and UNRWA for equipment, and hire workers. After considering the price of having tables made, we . . . purchased grass mats to place on the floor. On a trip to Jerusalem we bought five hundred spoons and some big pots. UNRWA provided thermos-type containers, plates, and a large primus burner for cooking which used kerosene. The senior medical officer in Hebron supplied us with lists of children to be served.[35]

After prolonged haggling over rent, the twins secured a shop as premises for distribution. When Hebron's chief of police gave them permission to purchase water, they hired a man with a donkey to haul the water in cans.[36]

Children arrived barefoot on the first day in the rain. Meals varied and could include dates, rice with laban (thickened yoghurt), tomatoes, bread, lentil soup, or vegetable soup with meat. When they received some cod liver oil, in order to supplement their diets with vitamins A and D, the children had to swallow it before they received food.[37]

The twins found out some of their employees had been arrested for stealing food and selling it. Ida went to the prison where the thieves were being held and found out they were poor themselves. As the twins required honest staff, they opted not to press charges, but let the dishonest employees go from their jobs.[38]

Many people went directly to the twins' home, asking for help. Even those who could buy food appeared, looking for handouts, so discernment was required. One elderly man who could barely lift his feet came with his young wife who was carrying a baby with the only arm she had. They had not eaten for a few days so the twins gave them food. Another time, a pregnant woman arrived with a suckling child, asking for baby clothes. A few days before, a parcel had arrived from a woman in the US whose baby son had died. She sent his clothes to Ida and Ada, asking that they be given to the poor, which they were able to do.[39]

When Ada and Ida learned of some shepherds who had been killed when they strayed across the Israeli border with their sheep, the twins decided to help their families who lived in caves with little prospect of earning money. Each received a lamb and ewe plus another sheep. They also helped several villages repair their cisterns and bought thousands of olive trees and grape vines for Arab farmers.[40]

Within five years, the twins and their team were feeding 1,700 children in five border villages and operating two milk centres in other villages. They provided milk for up to 125 babies at another feeding centre and distributed cooking oil as it became available, as well as special treats during Christmas.[41]

With all the critical aid they were providing and with so many people dependent on them, Ada and Ida were under constant pressure. They were able to spend some time away at a facility run by German Catholic nuns in the biblical town of Emmaus. While there, the twins spent many hours sitting beneath pine trees looking out towards the Mediterranean Sea. One of the other guests was a German Lutheran deaconess who ran a school for girls in Bethlehem. Ida longed for the MCC to open an orphanage and school, especially when she heard the Bethlehem school had 2,000 children on its waiting list.[42]

Orphanage

Ada and Ida continued to ponder how to care for children whose parents could not.[43] Women were raising children on their own, due to death, abandonment, or divorce. When women remarried, the new husband would not care for children from the first marriage.

Some women abandoned their families altogether because they could not bear to raise them as refugees.[44]

The twins visited nine orphanages and schools in the area before opening one of their own. Ada and Ida noticed the facilities were in areas with a sizeable percentage of Christians. Most of the children in them were Christians and were middle class. These institutions did not reach out to the Muslims who were the most needy.[45]

In 1954, Yuseif Sherif, a wealthy man from Hebron, offered to sell land to Ida and Ada to open a hospital or a church. Sherif made this offer to other Christians, but the twins and the MCC were the only ones to demonstrate interest. Sherif was a more liberal Muslim who thought the presence of a Christian institution would be a 'moderating force.' People in Hebron had respect for both the MCC and for the twins.[46] However, the sale could not be completed, as it was illegal for foreigners to own land. Instead they rented a house where they would accommodate and also teach boys. Before they even received permission, a Hebron official had ten boys for them.[47] Thus began the Mennonite Orphanage for Boys, later known as the Arab Evangelical Orphanage for Boys.

Ada and Ida hired staff and purchased beds, dishes, and desks. The house was beyond the city water system, so they used the house's cistern and later installed a water pump.[48] They rummaged through the MCC's donated items looking for bedding and curtains, as well as in the 150 bales of clothing from the ICC. The town mattress maker was hired and durable sandals were made from old tyres.[49] They hired a local Christian woman to be the matron, a Greek Orthodox woman to teach, a cook, and a cleaner. They began with boys who were five- to six-years-old. As these boys went to the next grade, other five- to six-year-olds were admitted.[50]

The first boy arrived in February 1955. His mother had died and his dad could not care for him. He was only five and arrived with a cold, so he was put to bed under three blankets, surrounded by seven empty beds.[51] Another boy went to the twins after living in an alley following his father's death. An aunt had looked out for him, but her husband drove the child out. Another boy lived with a baker and delivered bread to pay for his keep. He had strong shoulders from carrying a board on his head laden with loaves.[52] Soon they had nine boys, then thirteen, then twenty-eight.

One boy had been abandoned by his mother and then lived with some refugees as his father earned little money. While the boy was at the orphanage, his father came to take him home, to alleviate his own loneliness and have someone buy him cigarettes. The man examined the facilities and revealed he had heard the twins would keep his son and turn him into a priest. Ada and Ida reassured him they only wanted his son to study and find a good job. The father accepted his inability to provide clothes, food, and an education, so he departed in tears.[53]

Sunday was visitors' day. One time, two sons were overheard telling their father who came to visit he was using bad words.[54] Some families removed their boys and other boys took off on their own. The boys who ran away often returned and Ada and Ida accepted them, but if they ran off again, they were not readmitted.[55]

Other visitors included lice, at which point, everything was washed— 'boys, beds, clothing.' Measles, thankfully, was not something they dealt with, but the need for the dentist did arise. The 'alley kid' needed a lot of fillings and wept a lot.[56]

Boys were sent to a relative for two weeks at the end of the summer, during which time the staff also had a holiday. Many of the boys returned dirty, with bugs in their hair and sores on their arms and legs. Ada and Ida sometimes wished the boys had not left at all.[57]

All of the boys were given three meals a day, a dose of cod liver oil, and were tested for infections. They slept in clean beds, attended school, and felt and looked well. So, they were able to enjoy some outings.[58]

The Christian boys attended a Sunday school in Bethlehem. Some Muslim boys wanted to go as well, in which case the twins had to clarify it was the boys' choice.[59] All joined in day trips to the Dead Sea, the Jordan River, and the Mountain of Temptation, where one of the Arab teachers would tell the accompanying Bible stories. One time, the staff took some rope and made a swing, which the boys had not seen before. So, Ada and Ida had some playground equipment made, including swings, a seesaw, and a slide.[60]

At Christmas, the twins invited the boys to their home, which they had decorated with tinsel and old Christmas cards. They told the Christmas story using flannel graph (felt figures placed on a fabric background) and gave out candy and apples. On December 23, they decorated a tree and prepared small gifts and new clothes for each boy. The Christian boys learned Bible verses and retold them, then guests came for a presentation and party.

Two years later, the orphanage was relocated to larger premises, but they still did not have official permission from the government to teach.[61] Both the twins and the MCC refused to have Islam taught in the school. Complaints issued to the orphanage included teaching the children on the Muslim holy day, Friday, and teaching Christianity. As a compromise, the Muslim boys were sent to a government school to be taught Islam and a licence was finally granted.[62]

After five years in Hebron, Ada and Ida returned to the US for a year. They prayed for God to bless their efforts and 'forgive where [they] had failed.'[63] Life was different in the US and it was not possible to pick up where they had left off five years earlier. In Hebron, they were in charge and were decision makers, but in the US, life seemed 'trivial and unproductive.' They began to receive letters from Hebron with questions and problems.[64]

Bessie Plant, with the MCC, was left in charge in Hebron. When Bessie arrived for a time of transition, her lack of tact in relating to the public threatened the twins' years of hard-earned goodwill in the community. Bessie was also concerned that there were no obvious efforts to convert the students.[65] Along with others in the MCC, she was uncomfortable with a Mennonite facility in a largely Muslim area with few Christians [66] and tried to have it moved.

At that point, the orphanage had not yet been licensed to teach, so Bessie did not have the boys resume lessons and a new class was not admitted in the fall. Only thirteen boys remained, down from thirty-four, so Ida returned to Hebron early from her leave.[67] Upon her arrival, she contacted boys who had left and urged them to return, which many did.[68]

While most of the children who went to the orphanage and school were keen, some struggled to adjust. The facility was set up for boys, but one day a girl was brought to them by a policeman who insisted she be admitted. Her father had died, her mother remarried, so she lived with an abusive uncle who was recently imprisoned. She also had a crippled leg after a truck ran over her when she was younger. The girl stayed at the orphanage a month, but was eventually dismissed as she only communicated with violence and swearing and refused to change.[69]

A few other girls were subsequently enrolled. When two arrived, Ida took them to the storeroom to find some dresses. One of the girls remarked that while a particular dress fit, it was not pretty. Ida admitted to herself it was a true statement, but no words could convince the girl to don the dress.[70]

When Ada returned, she found out she had been made secretary of the ICC committee. This meant working one month for the MCC and one month for the ICC. During a meeting in Beirut, she stayed in an apartment that had such conveniences as hot water, central heating, and a fridge. If funds were available, Ada thought she would like to buy a new stove for the orphanage. She checked herself, though, wondering if she wanted things others had. At that point, she remembered Jesus, who had nowhere to lay his head.[71]

Major Changes

By 1966, the MCC leadership was changing. It was examining its commitment to the Hebron institution, as the focus of the MCC was on the provision of material aid. The twins were told to eliminate the lowest two classes as a first step towards closing down. But the institution was personal to Ada and Ida as they were sometimes the only source of stability in otherwise difficult lives.[72]

The twins received funds directly from three sources: their home church, a group of supporters in the US called the Jordan Club and from sponsors in the US and Canada who supported individual orphans. This enabled Ada and Ida to operate with some autonomy and was a factor in enabling the distance in the relationship with the MCC.[73] The twins linked up with the Evangelical Episcopal Church, and later, Holy Land Ministries.[74] The MCC continued to send blankets, canned meat, and other supplies to the orphanage, despite the severing of the administrative link.[75]

By the mid-1960s, people in Hebron had to practise for air raids. This involved blacking out any light, curfews, and street patrols. Ida painted a large red cross on a sheet and affixed it to the roof to indicate they were an institution. Soldiers camped on the orphanage's porch, rumours of wars and attacks swirled and tempers flared, resulting in gangs of men of all ages who were 'set on destruction.'[76]

Ada left Hebron in 1967 to care for the sisters' ailing mother in the US. At the end of the school year Ida gave out report cards before most of the boys left for the summer. Some had nowhere to go, so the boys stayed where they were. Within two days, the Six Day War commenced when Israel took control of the West Bank, including Hebron.[77]

Soldiers searched the orphanage property looking for weaponry, but only found 'boy-sized shoes' and other provisions. Shops remained open, but with few supplies. Jews flooded into Hebron to visit Abraham's tomb and other biblical sites, while many Arabs fled and were unable to return.[78]

Ida's challenges were myriad. Sending and receiving mail became more complicated, banking was complicated, and costs started rising. Also, the MCC had taken beds and other furniture as well as a vehicle and refrigerator to one of their schools. When the school year began, there was no shortage of needy boys. In November, the twins' mother died, which meant Ada returned to Hebron just in time for Christmas.[79]

Life changed under Israeli control with the arrival of Jewish settlers.[80] Routine provided some sense of order as Ida and Ada purchased grapes that they dried on the roof to make raisins.[81] The changes were not all bad, as the twins were now able to visit the biblical sites of Nazareth, Cana, and the Sea of Galilee.[82]

Peace was a distant prospect between Jews and Arabs with claim and counterclaim.[83] Ida wondered how life continued for many poor families who survived on very little. She and Ada recognised that while many struggled, the twins were always able to reach into their storeroom for what they needed.[84]

When Ida and Ada hired a Hebron man as principal, they were able to take a vacation together. He oversaw enrollment that year, which included five handicapped boys who moved around with crutches. No other school in the area would accommodate these boys. Ida's concerns that they would not integrate were not realised. Older boys helped them on the stairs and they joined in ball games, crutches and all.[85]

Curfews, roadblocks, and failed peace talks clouded many days. The year 1979 was particularly difficult for the orphanage, with a flu outbreak, a fire in the office, and a court case with their landlord. The twins paid an agreed amount of money for their premises, but with currency devaluation, the landlord wanted to increase the rent.[86] It would take nine years to satisfy both sides.[87]

Despite these concerns, the twins worked hard on the end of year festivities, which included a dramatisation of the biblical story of Ananias and Sapphira. The twins were keenly aware these presentations could be the only time the parents would hear Christian teaching, so they tried to make them memorable.[88] Ada and Ida were encouraged that year when a boy they had raised was baptised. They invited thirty guests for dinner and sent a goat to the bakery to be stuffed and cooked.[89]

'Some people urged us to close the school and leave the work. . . . When the days were cold, the checkbook almost empty,' according to Ada, 'and curfews kept us from buying bread and vegetables, we admit we were tempted. Then a knock on the door and a smiling face would greet us with, "Do you remember me?" and all doubts would fade.'[90] The twins would share memories with the visitor and listen to accounts of Bible stories told long ago.[91]

The twins displayed remarkable courage and endurance to survive 'more or less alone' in an almost entirely Muslim city. This is according to Gregg Doolittle, who worked with Ada and Ida for a year in the 1970s, and who now co-directs the Hebron school they founded. The twins were close and supported each other emotionally through the wars of 1956, 1967, 1973, and the first intifada in 1987.[92]

'We were glad to leave the cold buildings,' said Ida upon her retirement. 'The leaking roofs, the struggle to pay bills, and the many, many problems—it was the people we would miss.'[93]

By the time they retired in 1989, the twins had eighty-two boarders and fifty-eight day students.

The school remains in operation.

Ministry

It was the prayer of Ada and Ida that the people they sought to help could 'read the love of God' in the aid they distributed.[94]

The twins did put people in the way of the gospel. One of their early helpers contracted tuberculosis and was sent to a TB clinic run by Christians, where he heard the gospel and asked for prayer. 'Whether or not he accepted Jesus, I do not know,' wrote Ida, 'but I hoped his limited, child-like faith led him to a decision for Christ.'[95] The twins took Issa, one of their Muslim workers, to church in Bethlehem, along with his father-in-law for five years. When Ida and Ada invited their translator Mr Hammouri to the church, they were surprised to hear that he had long wished to attend church with them.[96]

For their first Christmas, the twins decorated their home with paper 'shepherds, wisemen, and bells.' As neighbours came by, the twins told them about Christ. They also gave New Testaments to their workers and other Christmas visitors.[97] During their second Christmas, they hosted some MCCers, workers, and neighbours, including a Christian family. The group sang and ate and Ada told the Christmas story. They continued to meet weekly and grew to forty-five attendees. One week, no one came; no one would admit that some Muslims had threatened anyone who attended.[98]

One of their boys returned ten years after graduating to say he was studying in the UK. He was involved in mission work to Arabs in the Netherlands and had been invited to join a missions team in India with Operation Mobilisation. The twins were grateful, especially as he had been a problem child. He suggested organising a reunion— sixteen boys came. At the event, he related his Christian testimony.[99]

During the Suez crisis in 1956, the US government urged non-essential workers to leave the Middle East. The twins packed up their belongings and went to a MCC meeting in Jerusalem. Some were convinced they should depart, while Ada and Ida had an equally strong commitment to stay. They felt their commitment was from the Lord, and 'He was able to keep and use us for His glory.'[100]

Ada and Ida prayed daily for each boy in their care and were certain that some followed Christ in secret. The twins heard of those who lived in Hebron as Muslims, but as Christians elsewhere. If they did not fast or stayed away from the mosque they were mistreated. 'We . . . rejoiced they had made commitments to the Lord and trusted He was guiding them in their decisions.'[101]

The twins attended the wedding of two secret Arab believers—the groom was a former student. After the marriage, the bride was baptised, as she was no longer under her Muslim father's rule. When the couple told the bride's father of their Christian faith, he disowned his daughter.[102]

One of their Muslim boys who spent most of his life in the school, including vacations, decided to become a Christian and asked to be baptised. When he told his family, he asked the twins for prayer, as his life might be in danger. His family did not oppose his choice, but did not want to hear about the gospel for themselves. The twins were in contact with him until he died and even though he had many struggles, he was faithful to the end.[103]

A former student named Majed continued to rely on help from Ada and Ida as an adult, but the twins were not able to find solutions for him. They came to realise Majed had mental and medical struggles. He often asked for prayer and after he died, Ida believed Majed had accepted Christ after hearing Bible stories from the twins and from other Christians.[104]

Singleness and Family

Ada and Ida and their Arab friends became like family, as their lives were so closely woven together.[105] When Ada died in 1995, a former student, Khalil M Amro, admitted he had never felt like an orphan until her death.[106]

The twins had a motherly concern for the children they cared for. A particularly sickly child was brought to them, whom they fed until he began to thrive. His mother told them many times the child was theirs because they saved his life.[107] Apart from caring for their regular students, the twins unofficially adopted three boys. Ida and Ada worked, sacrificed, and struggled to be good mothers to these boys.[108]

Arab society has rules for how men and women interact. It was highly unusual that Ida and Ada had a foot in the world of both men and women.[109] When they were setting up their first milk centre, Ida spent a day with several men, including soldiers, religious leaders, the local school master, and police. At lunchtime, Ida was ushered to another room, but opted to eat with the men from her own plate of food, while the others shared a platter. Either they were being polite or she was 'brazen,' but she had spent a lot of time with them that day so there was no point in eating alone.[110]

Without husbands, the twins were honoured in ways reserved for men. At the home of their long-time interpreter Mr Hammouri, they were served an entire lamb. Ada recounts:

> I watched as my host piled my plate high with rice and pieces of all parts of the lamb—even a bit of brains and tongue. Perhaps because an animal has only two eyes, they are considered a delicacy. I discovered they are not as grisly as I imagined. . . .[111]

In Arab society, most women marry. The twins wrote to their mother about this, clarifying this 'only applies to the natives.'[112] Being women on their own had its advantages. During the election in 1954 all transport ceased to prevent people voting twice. Ada and Ida moved freely. 'We were foreigners, and we were women . . . so we were no threat.'[113]

After Ada died, Ida lived another nine years at a retirement home in Pennsylvania, US. In retirement, she volunteered at a nursing facility— ever helpful until the end. Ida was thrilled when students or staff visited, wrote or called her from across the world.[114] She died in 2004 after a brief illness.

Endnotes

1. Marie E. Cutman, *We Sat Where They Sat: Ada and Ida Stoltzfus Thirty-Seven and One Half Years in the Ancient City of Hebron* (Morgantown: Masthof Press, 1996), 194.

2. ibid., xiv.

3. ibid., 78.

4. Susanna J. Stoltzfus, "God Blessed Their Hands: Ada and Ida Stoltzfus's Fifteen Years in Hebron in MCC Service: 1952–1967" (Goshen: Mennonite Historical Library, 2003), 4.

5. ibid., 5.

6. Cutman, *We Sat Where They Sat,* xiv.

7. Gregg Doolittle, email, 4 October 2020.

8. Aileen Coleman, author interview, 26 September 2020.

9. *We Sat Where They Sat*, p. 11

10. ibid., 12.

11. ibid., 13.

12. ibid., 18.

13. ibid., 11.

14. ibid.

15. ibid., 156.

16. ibid., 8–9.

17. ibid., 18.

18. ibid., 9–10.

19. ibid., 19.

20. ibid.

21. ibid., 22.

22. ibid., 19.

23. ibid.

24. ibid., 23–24.

25. ibid., 25.

26. ibid., 27.

27. ibid., 75.

28. ibid., 28.

29. ibid.

30. ibid., 31–32.

31. ibid., 33–34.

32. ibid., 35.

33. ibid., 36.

34. ibid., 37.

35. ibid.

36. ibid., 39.

37. ibid.
38. ibid., 40.
39. ibid., 53.
40. ibid., 92–93, 96.
41. ibid., 45.
42. ibid., 70.
43. ibid., 41.
44. ibid., 105.
45. Stoltzfus, "God Blessed Their Hands," 24.
46. ibid., 20.
47. *We Sat Where They Sat*, 108.
48. ibid.
49. ibid., 110.
50. "God Blessed Their Hands," 28.
51. *We Sat Where They Sat*, 111.
52. ibid., 114.
53. ibid., 117–118.
54. ibid., 113.
55. ibid., 114–115.
56. ibid., 115.
57. ibid., 116.
58. ibid., 119.
59. ibid., 155.
60. ibid., 119.
61. ibid., 127.
62. ibid., 133.
63. ibid., 129.
64. ibid.
65. "God Blessed Their Hands," 25.
66. ibid., 2.
67. ibid., 26.
68. *We Sat Where They Sat*, 134.
69. ibid.
70. ibid., 149.
71. ibid., 140.
72. ibid., 178.
73. "God Blessed Their Hands," 2, 28.
74. *We Sat Where They Sat*, 178.
75. *We Sat Where They Sat*, 256.

76. *We Sat Where They Sat*, 188.
77. ibid.
78. ibid., 194–195.
79. ibid., 201–203.
80. ibid., 206.
81. ibid., 208.
82. ibid., 207.
83. ibid., 210.
84. ibid., 212.
85. ibid., 258.
86. ibid., 259.
87. ibid., 277.
88. ibid., 260.
89. ibid., 262.
90. ibid., 291.
91. ibid., 284.
92. Doolittle, email.
93. *We Sat Where They Sat*, 310.
94. ibid., 93.
95. ibid., 41.
96. ibid., 88.
97. ibid., 46.
98. ibid., 89.
99. ibid., 179–180.
100. ibid., 83.
101. ibid., 291.
102. ibid., 292.
103. ibid., 222.
104. ibid., 280.
105. ibid., 284.
106. ibid., 312.
107. ibid., 103.
108. Doolittle, email.
109. ibid.
110. *We Sat Where They Sat*, 36.
111. ibid., 57.
112. ibid., 53.
113. ibid., 79.
114. ibid., 311.

Aileen Coleman

The new mother presented Aileen with the roasted sheep's eyeball. Seated at a feast hosted by a grateful sheikh's wife, who had given birth to a son with Aileen's help, she eyed the prized morsel. Mercifully it was a small sheep, so Aileen popped it into her mouth and swallowed it whole.[1]

Early Life and Call

Born in Bundaberg, Southern Queensland, Australia in 1930, Aileen was the youngest of seven children. Some labelled her a rebel, but Aileen preferred 'adventurous'[2] and a 'party girl.'[3]

At the age of twenty-one, she attended an evangelistic meeting while at college in Bundaberg and responded to God's call on her life.[4] She went straight to Melbourne Bible Institute, which was a 'shock' to her and 'a shock to the Bible school,' going from being 'sort of wild' to being a missionary, with the goal of translating the Bible in the Pacific region.[5]

At Bible school, she was given 'the worst assignment in the school,' which was to write about the Muslim world. In the 1950s, few missionaries were working with Muslims, but she did discover an American agency and heard about Dr Sarah Hosmon in Sharjah, present day UAE, who was running a midwifery clinic. Dr Hosmon responded to Aileen's queries, then asked Aileen to mobilise her school to pray that the Lord would send them a nurse with post-graduate midwifery training. Aileen started to pray for 'a nurse who had my qualification,' then went herself, answering her own prayer.[6]

Aileen's decision to go to the Middle East was not universally embraced. Family, friends and some at her Bible school told her,

'Single women don't do that,' but at the age of twenty-five, Aileen was certain this was what she should do. She has never regretted her decision, knowing from the beginning that her place was 'with the Muslim people.'[7]

Sharjah, 1955–1957

In 1955, Aileen joined Dr Hosmon in Sharjah, northeast of Dubai. Although wealthy now, Sharjah was impoverished and needy when Aileen arrived. Obstetrics were basic—new mothers' vaginas were packed with salt to stop bleeding, resulting in pain and scarring. The locals did not yet trust these western-trained medical practitioners. So, only the most desperate cases were brought to the hospital where the staff sought to unpick damage caused by local midwives. Aileen delivered babies at all hours, only sleeping 'between contractions.'[8]

Sometimes the mother died during delivery. In one case, the mother's low haemoglobin, malaria, and earlier wounds culminated in her bleeding to death. Aileen was overcome and retreated in tears, uttering she had reached her limit. A senior missionary found Aileen and asked why she had come. 'Don't you want to help these women? If you don't, who will?' The words were harsh, but served as a crossroads. Aileen was determined not to quit.[9]

Further challenges awaited the novice medical missionary. A local woman entered the Sharjah hospital after being in labour for six days. She was nearing death, a Caesarean section was required, and Dr Hosmon was bedridden with tuberculosis (TB). Dr Hosmon declared to Aileen, 'This lady is dying. If you don't try to help her, she will die. If you do try, she may die, but then again she might live.' She gave the terrified Aileen a surgical manual, who propped up the book in the operating room, then 'read and cut, and read and cut.' While a family member looked on, the baby was delivered, Aileen completed the procedure and both mother and baby survived. The locals were impressed Aileen could read, and she became known as 'Doctorah who does everything "by the book."'[10]

Arroub: 1957–1965

Aileen moved from Sharjah to Bethlehem in 1957 to stay with a missionary couple while taking an Arabic course in Jerusalem offered by the University of London (UK). Her Arabic improved, and when she chastised some Arab children who were begging for money, one of them warned his friends, 'the tall one . . . looks American, but she is really an Arab.'[11]

The director of nurses at Baraka Tuberculosis Hospital in nearby Arroub was going on home assignment and Aileen was asked to fill her shoes for six months. The director did not return, so Aileen agreed to stay until a replacement was found. She ended up remaining at Baraka for eight years and starting a nursing school.[12] During her time there, she made three important advances for her future work.

Eleanor

First, Aileen met Dr Eleanor Soltau, the medical director at Baraka, who was in the same mission agency as Aileen. Eleanor was an American respiratory doctor and had been raised in Korea where her parents were missionaries. She was fourteen years older than Aileen and became her mentor. Aileen learned a lot from Eleanor about 'persevering [and] praying.'[13] The two women would become ministry partners for the next forty years.

Strategy

Second, while at Baraka, Aileen recognised that 'midwifery is not too beneficial for evangelism,' because the mother's sole interest is her newborn.[14] In contrast, the treatment of a chronic disease like TB was advantageous for Muslim evangelism, as adequate treatment requires a stay of one to two months or longer in a sanatorium. During their stay, patients are educated about their TB and receive drugs that are administered over a period of time. This grants the missionaries opportunities to become acquainted with their patients on a deeper level. The patients would come to trust the staff, and share 'their problems, the joys, and the heartbreaks.'[15] Aileen and Eleanor also had first-hand experience with TB, both having had the disease twice—one of Eleanor's bouts resulted in the removal of one of her lungs.[16]

During extended stays at the sanatorium Aileen and Eleanor later opened in Jordan, relationships deepened more often with men than women.[17] Some women did respond, including one who was unable to conceive. With treatment, she bore a son and despite staff praying and witnessing to her, she did not accept the gospel. When her young son died two years later, Aileen dreaded the visit to the bereaved mother. But when Aileen summoned the courage to call on the grief-stricken woman, she found her sitting alone. The two women wept as they watched a shepherd coaxing his sheep across a small stream. When the shepherd placed the lambs on the other side of the flowing water, the ewes found their way across. Just then, the bereaved mother's tears flowed even more. She relayed to Aileen because of her hesitancy in accepting God through Jesus, He had placed her 'little lamb' on the other side, 'in order that I would want to be with him badly enough to come to God His way.' She asked to hear the gospel again, a request Aileen lovingly and humbly honoured.[18]

Bedouin

Third, she encountered and came to love the Bedouin, the Arab desert dwellers. These nomadic people shift their woven goat hair tents to higher ground in summer and to lower ground in winter, along with their families, animals, and vehicles. Today, many are more settled, yet Bedouin values and traditions endure in the Arab world. City dwellers in the Gulf spend weekends camping in their desert tents during cooler months, and substantial villas sit alongside a tent where visitors are received.

Much of what Aileen knew about the Bedouin she learned from her correspondence with Sir John Glubb. Glubb Pasha, as he was known, led the Arab Legion from 1938 until 1956, which later became the Royal Jordanian Army. In her letters to him, Aileen urged him to pen a book about the Arab tribes.[19]

Aileen sought to live as the Bedouin, as long as this did not contradict Scripture.[20] She lauded Bedouin family structures: children respected their elders and adults cared for their parents. Aileen also admired their simple lives with few belongings, musing what they might think of homes in the west crammed with stuff.[21]

The famed Bedouin hospitality is unequalled and Aileen witnessed them sharing precious resources with visitors. When she and Eleanor later moved to Jordan, they visited an impoverished Bedouin mother and her five children. The tent was in shreds, a few blankets served as furnishings and there was no food to be seen.[22] Yet, the mother offered each woman an egg. The missionaries refused, but the mother insisted, saying, 'You told me about Jesus Christ, and He has been with me ever since I repented and accepted Him. . . . I have no other way of giving a gift to Him who loved me and died for me.'[23]

During her many years among the Bedouin, Aileen found them uncomplaining, despite their hardships. This was partly due to their Islamic faith—their circumstances were the will of Allah so they were content.[24]

Although Bedouin are not open to outsiders, they came to appreciate and respect Aileen and Eleanor. The Bedouin made Aileen and Eleanor blood brothers by actually blending a small amount of blood, thereby cementing a commitment to mutual protection.[25] When Aileen was in a serious car accident in 1996, she received 'fifteen units of Muslim blood, just like that' in a culture where Muslims are hesitant to donate blood. When the Arabs heard it was for their doctorah, they gave. 'They're my kinsmen,' she maintains.[26]

Following a split in their church denomination, Aileen and Eleanor were asked to leave Baraka.[27] As most Bedouins were located east of the Jordan River, they crossed over in 1965 to what is today the country of Jordan to pursue their dream of establishing a TB sanatorium for Bedouins.[28]

Jordan, 1965–present day

Aileen and Eleanor travelled to the US to share their vision. They 'naively' thought their friends and supporters would be 'happy and enthusiastic' about their new venture. Instead, they found the idea of 'two women . . . doing things that usually only men did'[29] in the Arab world to be a non-starter. Several mission agencies turned them down because 'women don't start things in the Middle East.' Others said they would pray for the women, Aileen recalled—a polite way of saying no.[30]

The two women received a contrasting reception from their friend Roy Gustafson. He asked if they were 'just bent out of shape' after being 'kicked out of' Baraka. They assured him they were not, but believed this was what the Lord wanted them to do. 'Well,' he said, 'what are you doing sitting in my living room?'[31] Roy read Ecclesiastes 11:4,6 – 'He who observes the wind will not sow. . . . In the morning sow your seed . . . for you do not know which will prosper, this or that'

(ESV). He challenged them to carry on: 'If you're so convinced that this is what God wants you to do,' then 'get up and do it.' So they did.[32]

First Premises

The mid-1960s witnessed a lot of political unrest in Jordan and the wider region. Local people whom Aileen and Eleanor 'really admired' advised against proceeding with their sanatorium. A few encouraged them, including Shukri Qawas, who was originally opposed to foreign missionaries, thinking the Arabs should be evangelising their own people.[33]

Before opening their doors, Aileen and Eleanor needed permission from Jordan's ministry of health. Local friends told Aileen and Eleanor that the minister of health was a fanatic and was aware they wanted to open a Christian facility where they wanted to evangelise. After a lot of praying, they went to inform the minister what they wished to do. He gazed at them for what 'seemed like forever,' then said, 'Thank you very much. How can I help you?' He even sent one of his doctors with them to look for suitable premises.[34]

The two women settled on Mufraq in the north of Jordan near the Syrian border with $50 between them. Looking around for a suitable location, they saw only one brick and mortar structure and the landlord wanted $1,000 dollars for the annual rent. Just then, a cheque arrived in the mail—a forgotten investment of Eleanor's—for $1,100. Six months later, following a lot of scrubbing, the sixteen-bed facility opened, furnished with donated medical equipment.[35] Besides caring for patients, Eleanor did the laundry and Aileen did the cooking.[36]

At first the Bedouins did not trust the new arrivals, preferring their own ways. The Bedouin treated tummy aches by sewing the stomach with string, branded flesh to inhibit disease, and wore amulets for protection. One by one, though, patient numbers grew, with publicity via word of mouth or the 'desert telegraph.' Because Aileen and Eleanor shared the gospel and prayed with each patient, their institution became known as the 'preaching hospital.'[37]

Some fanatical Jordanians opposed the sanatorium from the outset. They questioned the motivation of the missionaries, espousing that they worked for the CIA, were making piles of money, or were Israeli spies. If Aileen and Eleanor had not been so occupied by their work, or 'convinced this is where they should be,' then 'it could have been discouraging.'[38]

Two years after Aileen and Eleanor moved to Mufraq, the Six Day War saw Israeli jets attack an adjacent air base. The 1967 war brought bereavement to local families[39] and 'the grief and anguish seemed to be never-ending,' according to Aileen. The strife deepened the level of poverty, causing some to live beneath a tree or in a cave.[40]

During the 1970 Jordanian civil war, Aileen and Eleanor were instructed to leave the country, but they declined. The Palestine Liberation Organisation (PLO) entered the area and stole the women's vehicles. Aileen 'heckled them almost every day' in an attempt to retrieve their property. Her repeated visits to the PLO base built up a rapport and one day, in exasperation, Aileen took hold of one of the young men and said that as they had the women's vehicles, they must do the shopping.[41] Amazingly, they did, but if it was not good quality, Aileen demanded 'better stuff.'[42]

Aileen and Eleanor learned that one of their absconded vehicles was in Syria. As the only non-American, it fell to Aileen to retrieve it—Americans were not allowed to enter Syria due to the current political climate. She boarded a public bus with broken windows, clad in a 'too-large trench coat' and 'permanently out-of-date' scarf. Children wondered aloud who this foreigner was until the driver stopped the bus and thanked the 'Soviet woman' who had come to Syria and did not dress like a tourist. Aileen did recoup the vandalised truck, for which they were grateful.[43]

Many years later during the 1990 Gulf War, Aileen cautioned their foreign staff to avoid demonstrations. While doing some errands in Amman, Aileen's vehicle was suddenly encircled by protestors crying, 'death to all westerners.' When one of them managed to open her car door, they wondered aloud who could speak to this woman in English. Aileen asked in Arabic, 'What do you want to tell me?' When he said her skirt was hanging outside of the car door, Aileen thanked him profusely.[44]

Halfway through their eight years in the rented building, Aileen and Eleanor acknowledged the need for more room. They spoke to the Lord about money and to their supporters about their vision.[45] Yet, how to construct a bigger structure?[46]

Lester and a New Sanatorium

'I can't do much of anything.' So wrote American Lester Gates in a letter to Aileen in 1965, after hearing her speak. He offered to help with maintenance, saying he could 'Perhaps, build better cupboards than you or Eleanor.'[47]

Lester went to Jordan as a self-supporting volunteer at the age of fifty-six. Soon after arriving, he asked Aileen and Eleanor why they did not build a bigger facility. Around that time, a friend of Eleanor's sent them $1,000, recommending they purchase property. With his farmer's eye, Lester looked around for land with a rocky foundation and access to precious water. He found both and for $2,000 the fledglings bought '25 acres of desert.'[48] Herb Klassen, who would later run the sanatorium, noted that the building of 'such a substantial building in the middle of the desert' was a 'huge step of faith,' especially as there was 'nothing else around them.'[49]

Aileen had huge admiration for Lester, who 'gave every part of his body and his wealth.' He did not finish high school, and needed Aileen's help to compose official correspondence. Yet, he was 'intelligent and [a] talented builder.'[50]

Aileen recognised that sleeping in a sanatorium would be the first time the Bedouins had not slept in a tent. So, to avoid the Bedouins feeling 'locked in,' each room had its own window.[51] The hospital was not heated, lest the patients become unused to unheated tent life.[52]

Al-Noor ('the light') Sanatorium was constructed with the help of summer volunteers who were 'a great help,' according to Aileen, including Franklin Graham, who would later chair the board of Al-Noor. The volunteers were 'frustrating at times,' yet it was gratifying to see the Lord at work in their lives, she mused.[53] A recent architecture graduate from the US, Raymond Luley researched Arab design and volunteered his services to prepare drawings for the hospital.[54] Fifteen years later accommodation for nurses, single women missionaries, and female staff was built.[55]

Funding came from varied sources. Aileen and Eleanor's friend Roy Gustafson led tours to the region and invited them to speak to his tour groups to raise funds. The Billy Graham Association also donated funds to the hospital, as did Lester Gates.[56] Later, Al-Noor charged patients $7 a month.[57]

Due to the various conflicts, including the Six-Day war of 1967, the 1970 civil war, and Yom Kippur in 1973, supplies were hard to come by. Lester was beaten up and kicked out of Jordan and when he returned, further construction was ill advised. Yet the building work continued and by 1973 Al-Noor Sanatorium for Chest Diseases was complete.[58]

Up and Running

Aileen and Eleanor saw God's provision for them, sometimes in dramatic ways. One of Aileen's responsibilities was to order medications for Al-Noor from the Netherlands every six months. As the delivery time drew close, she would write to the supplier to confirm the delivery. One time she sent a letter to verify her order, only to be told they had not received it. She quickly re-ordered, but delivery would take months. Al-Noor would have to close without the required medications, so Aileen and Eleanor prayed, while thinking of other options.

As their medications dwindled and the time was near to send all patients home, a staff member informed Aileen medications from a local source had been delivered. Aileen shooed them away, as she had not ordered anything from within Jordan, but the staff member insisted. Al-Noor had lent TB medications to the United Nations High Commission for Refugees a long time before, and they had chosen that day to deliver replacements. Miraculously, the medications they received were precisely what they had ordered from the Netherlands.[59]

While Aileen and Eleanor were at Baraka, they became acquainted with Nasri Khoury and his wife Manahi Hada who were student nurses. This couple migrated to Mufraq with Aileen and Eleanor and Nasri became the prime evangelist. He cared for patients as if they were family, so much so that when they recovered sufficiently, they willingly attended the daily Christian meetings.[60]

Nasri assisted Aileen to safeguard their focus on ministry to the Bedouin. He was also a key link with government officials, indispensable in untangling difficult situations that were beyond the reach of foreigners.[61] Aileen recalled seeing six Bedouin women clinging to Nasri during a war, 'asking for his protection.'[62]

Local women were recruited to train as nurses from nearby communities. Many who came forward had never slept in a bed, so they did not see the need to make patients' beds daily. This presented challenges for their tutelage, but the trainees did learn to exhibit care and love, weeping when cherished babies were released back to their families.[63]

Al-Noor attracted the attention of royalty, particularly Princess Zein, a cousin of Jordan's former monarch King Hussein. She was already an advocate for the Bedouin when she first heard of Al-Noor. She visited Al-Noor incognito, but was not allowed in as it was rest time. Aileen apologised in a later phone call, but Princess Zein communicated her admiration for the keeping of rules.[64] When asked why she supported the work of Christian missionaries in Jordan, Princess Zein said she had no trouble standing with those who exhibited 'love, compassion, and healing mercy to my people.'[65]

Aileen attributes her deepening understanding of the Bedouin to time spent with Princess Zein. The two women delivered aid and clothes to the Bedouin, sometimes in the throes of a snowstorm. Princess Zein summoned help from the army during a particularly severe tempest, working 'tirelessly [herself] ... from dawn until dusk.'[66]

In 1990, Princess Zein challenged Aileen and Eleanor to establish a clinic in the south of Jordan, as the Bedouin there could not afford the 185 miles bus trip to Al-Noor.[67] Eleanor was seventy-four and particularly enthusiastic and eventually moved to the south herself.[68] So, Princess Zein found a disused tourist guest house in Raas al-Naqb, which was converted into a clinic along with a small apartment. An old police fort was renovated for use by the clinic staff and volunteers.[69] Aileen continued to visit her old friend two days a week, sometimes joining Eleanor in a mobile clinic to visit the Bedouin tents.[70]

Home and Family

Aileen travelled outside of Jordan occasionally to speak about Al-Noor and to visit supporters. Upon her return, she noted the smell of fine perfume had been replaced by 'unwashed bodies and wet babies . . . the smell of home.'[71]

Aileen and Eleanor initially lived in the hospital and later in the nurses' residence. They welcomed cats, including at one time, Toots, who slept on various beds. One night, Aileen welcomed the warm furry animal nuzzled in her neck. In her drowsiness, Aileen worked out that Toots had long hair and this animal had short hair. She turned on the light to discover she had been cuddling a sizeable rat, but did not scream - 'there was no point.'[72]

Although Aileen did not bear children, she did care for nine Bedouin babies whose mothers had died.[73] In one case, a father pleaded with Aileen to care for his twin baby boys, but she did not think she could care for two, so Eleanor said she would help. The boys weighed three pounds (1.36 kilograms) or less, were unwell, and stayed at Al-Noor for two and a half years before being returned to their tents. The twins visited Al-Noor weekly, where they continued with Bible study.[74]

Baby Noorah was another waif who was brought to Al-Noor at three days old. She was likely poisoned at three months by visiting relatives, but 'was spared,' Aileen believes, 'to grow up to know Him.' Aileen kept a pink dress for Noorah to wear during her visits after she was returned to her desert life.[75]

Aileen views her singleness as an asset 'every day.' She had time for language study, visiting, and for meeting people. 'As a single person,' she said, 'you don't have the burden of a family. It's just been a blessing,'[76] and she did not have to make those 'wretched double beds.'[77]

However at times, her marital status was a hindrance to Aileen's life and ministry in that 'too many' men wanted to marry her.[78] While at Bible college, she was engaged to a fellow student, but Aileen's call to the Muslim world did not correspond with his, so they broke off their engagement. Two Arab Christian ministers wanted to marry Aileen, but the cultural restraints that would result prompted her to break off the relationships. Even later in life, an American businessman wooed her for two years, but to no avail.[79]

Transitions

In 1997, Eleanor was staying at the Al-Noor guest house in Mufraq. Her skirt caught fire from a kerosene heater and she died later in hospital from her burns, aged 81.[80] Aileen visited her in hospital, accompanied by her friend Princess Zein, who asked Aileen if Eleanor had died peacefully because of her work. Aileen relayed the essence of the gospel: 'We're not saved because we serve; we serve because we're saved.' Around five hundred people attended Eleanor's funeral, two-thirds of whom were Muslims.[81]

For Aileen, Eleanor's death was like losing her right arm.[82] Yet, Aileen has remained in her adopted country, praying, encouraging and loving. Even in her later years, she cared for an illegitimate baby boy, whose mother Nasri and Menahi had helped to escape certain death. He was given to a Jordanian Christian couple who did not have children of their own.[83]

Leadership of the hospital transitioned from Aileen in 2009 to Scott Hughett, and then to Herb Klassen in 2013.[84] At the time of writing, Aileen still preaches to the women patients twice a week, and hopes to visit some supporting churches in the US. Her favourite job, though, is 'sitting out in the dirt in a tent'[85] with women who confess to being

Christian believers in the past or those who are hostile to Christian teachings. They all need to hear the gospel.

Aileen recognises she will not live to see the establishment of the church among the Bedouins. But, 'it'll come . . . I have hope.'[86]

Endnotes

1. Annette Adams, *The Desert Rat* (Lafayette: Huntingdon House Publishers, 2022), 62.

2. ibid., 26.

3. Aileen Coleman, author interview, 26 September 2020.

4. Adams, *The Desert Rat*, 26–27.

5. Coleman, interview.

6. ibid.

7. ibid.

8. *The Desert Rat*, 28.

9. ibid., 29.

10. *The Desert Rat*, 30.

11. ibid., 31.

12. Coleman, interview.

13. ibid.

14. ibid.

15. *The Desert Rat*, 72.

16. ibid., 92.

17. ibid., 72.

18. ibid., 73–74.

19. ibid., 84–85.

20. ibid., 60.

21. ibid., 61.

22. ibid., 59.

23. ibid., 60.

24. ibid., 59.

25. ibid., 64.

26. Coleman, interview.

27. ibid..

28. *The Desert Rat*, 33.

29. *The Desert Rat*, 34.

30. Coleman, interview.

31. ibid.

32. *The Desert Rat*, 34.

33. Coleman, interview.

34. ibid.

35. *The Desert Rat*, 35.

36. Coleman, interview.

37. *The Desert Rat*, 35.

38. Coleman, interview.

39. *The Desert Rat*, 85.

40. ibid., 86.

41. ibid.

42. ibid., 87.

43. ibid., 87–88.

44. ibid., 89.

45. ibid., 35.

46. ibid., 40.

47. ibid., 39.

48. ibid., 40–41.

49. Herb Klassen, email, 1 January 2022.

50. Coleman, interview.

51. *The Desert Rat*, 42.

52. ibid., 57.

53. ibid., 43.

54. ibid., 42.

55. ibid., 44.

56. ibid., 43.

57. ibid., 62.

58. ibid., 41–42.

59. Klassen, email.

60. *The Desert Rat*, 48.

61. ibid., 48.

62. ibid., 47.

63. ibid., 48–49.

64. ibid., 50.

65. ibid., 54.

66. ibid., 52.

67. ibid., 77.

68. ibid.

69. ibid., 78.

70. ibid., 79.

71. ibid., 69.

72. ibid., 58.

73. ibid., 91.

74. ibid., 92.

75. ibid., 93.

76. Coleman, interview.

77. *The Desert Rat*, 28.
78. Coleman, interview.
79. *The Desert Rat*, 27–28.
80. ibid., 101–102.
81. ibid., 103.
82. ibid., 107.
83. ibid., 112.
84. Klassen, email.
85. Coleman, interview.
86. ibid.

Current Crop

Legions of single women continue to venture into the Arab world with the gospel. Today they are sharing Christian truths with their friends, neighbours, and colleagues. Following are portraits of eight contemporary women who are actively serving Christ in the Arab world.

Susanna

Susanna is from Europe, quadrilingual and completed a graduate degree in one of her three 'second' languages. She is also disabled. Many tried to talk her out of missionary work, but they became used to her being 'a bit special.'

North Africans came into focus for Susanna while she was working in France. When a door opened for ministry in North Africa, she rolled through it in her wheelchair. Locals began asking her where they could procure a wheelchair, so Susanna established a charity for disabled people and hired North Africans to work alongside her. It was a delight to her for disabled people to gain access to wheelchairs and other mobility aids.

When some North Africans took over the charity without Susanna's knowledge, she stepped back from the charity. Some associates said she was attempting to convert people, which made visa renewal difficult. While it was hard to relinquish her work with the charity, the Lord opened up other ministry opportunities and Susanna is seeing spiritual fruit. A few people in whom she invested are reading Scripture and showing interest in Christian teaching.

Susanna has remained in North Africa and is now helping in a French-speaking church. One of her aims is to mobilise the church to reach out to Arabs in Jesus' name. Some Africans are responding to this and a group of believers meets in her home, which is a 'great joy.'

'Being a single disabled person in a wheelchair from Europe,' has gained Susanna respect from Muslim men. While she is free to focus on ministry, singleness does have its drawbacks. She sees that younger women are pursued by men and 'approached in inappropriate ways.' It can also be a challenge to work exclusively with women.

Other single women who ministered in North Africa, like Lilias Trotter, inspire her. Susanna has never regretted her decision, as she had a clear calling and a 'deep peace' because she is where the Lord wants her to be.

Susanna has been particularly helped by these Bible verses.

Have I not commanded you? Be strong and courageous. Do not be frightened, and do not be dismayed, for the LORD your God is with you wherever you go. Joshua 1:9

For I know the plans I have for you, declares the LORD, plans for welfare and not for evil, to give you a future and a hope. Jeremiah 29:11

Nora

It is normal for Christians to share their faith according to Nora, citing Romans 10:14: *How are they to believe in him of whom they have never heard?* So she resolved to attend Bible college for a year following her nursing studies in her home country of the UK and then go overseas.

Four months into Nora's Bible college course, a mission mobiliser presented the pressing need for professionals 'right now' in the Arab world. After plenty of prayer, she felt God was calling her, so she completed her studies and her church commissioned her to go to the Arab world as a nurse.

While Nora has not regretted her decision, her first taxi ride in the Middle East made her wonder what she had done. She held on for dear life in the back and could not look out the window while asking the Lord why he 'brought me all the way out here to die at the hands of crazy drivers?!'

Nora began work immediately in a busy intensive care unit, 'where many patients were dying.' While seeking to speak into end-of-life issues, she gained insights into Arab culture. Arabs do not speak of death because anyone who does so is viewed as wishing to kill that person. She wanted to communicate 'the love and hope of Christ' to the families, but did not have the language ability and could not use the hospital translators. With her limited Arabic, Nora shared the 'hope of heaven' which was well received. Her male Muslim colleagues told her she had a 'different spirit' from other nurses and was 'genuine and kind.' Some staff would summon Nora to the side of weeping mothers to sit with them on the floor and hug them.

The mother of one of Nora's patients once asked if she believed in demons. When Nora said yes, the mother shared for an hour about demonic attacks. Nora told her the name of Jesus was powerful to overcome demons, which brought tears to the woman's eyes.

Nora loves to visit Arab families who exhibit such generous hospitality. Arab ladies like to watch her eat, she recounts, then they 'pinch my cheeks and tell me how cute I am.' Conversations soon turn to heaven's blessings alongside life's challenges. When a patient's husband brought her to visit Nora, the patient told Nora she was about to have an MRI scan. The husband had told Nora to encourage his wife not to be afraid, so Nora read aloud some Bible verses about anxiety.

Being single gives Nora 'freedom and flexibility' which are useful as she seeks to form new relationships. She is only constrained by her work schedule and her energy level. Locals do think it is odd she is not married and some seek to match Nora up with a son or brother.

Nora continues to be inspired by those working in 'difficult and closed countries.' She finds support from her mentor who worked in Asia and now leads a ministry to newcomers in the UK.

I can do all things through him who strengthens me. Philippians 4:13

Love is patient and kind. 1 Corinthians 13:4

Majida

Majida is an Arab. She is not a former Muslim—her family comes from ancient Christian roots.

Majida has ministered to Arab Muslim women in Europe for over twenty-five years. For many years she corresponded with men and women who were moved when they learned of Christian truths via Arabic Christian media, whether radio programmes, television shows via satellite, or Christian books and literature. This included a woman in Saudi Arabia, who went silent when her father killed her for being a Christian.

Presently, Majida is ministering to Arab women in a large European city, some of whom are recent arrivals. She has found out that when North Africans come to Europe, they perceive Christianity as weak and sidelined because churches are empty. They take refuge in their identity as Muslims.

Occasionally Majida visits the women in North Africa with whom she used to correspond. When she is there, the reality of Islam is all encasing—most people are Muslims and the call to prayer resounds five times every day. Friday is the common day off and during Ramadan life changes as people fast during the day and feast at night.

Single workers face challenges like loneliness, observes Majida, whether in the Arab world or in Europe. Without a man to accompany single women, local men bother them. This can be an opportunity to speak to those men about Christian things and single workers do have more time than families or couples.

Elise

Elise was born into a 'newly-formed Christian home' in the US, replete with 'Christian friends, missionaries, a children's Bible club, and our house group.' She read a lot of books about missions and thought she would end up overseas herself. Elise's family supported some missionaries in Morocco, so she heard a lot about North Africa.

At school, Elise's knowledge of North Africa continued to grow. An English teacher suggested she study Carthage, an important early Christian hub in Tunisia. Church history excited Elise and as her French teacher was actually from France, she had a head start on language. At Elise's Bible college, a missionary widow on staff ran a prayer group for North Africa Mission. Many who attended would go on to serve the Lord in North Africa and France.

Soon after Bible college, Elise landed a teaching job in Morocco, where a lovely believer helped her with language and evangelism. Along with colleagues from across North Africa, Elise enjoyed organising and putting on an inter-agency camp ministry for local children.

From Morocco, Elise went to Algeria where she saw 'amazing times' of open missionary work, extensive media output, and church growth. She lived with an Algerian family and as a team they travelled monthly to Algiers as well as occasionally to the east. Some stayed in *Dar Naama*, the villa that served as the base for the Algiers Mission Band, Lilias Trotter's agency. The team had plenty of 'amazing times' with teens, such as sea baptisms and an active deliverance ministry. They enjoyed fun times together and 'functioned well as a team—no lone workers.'

By the mid-1970s, North African countries were independent from France. Elise and her colleagues could no longer work openly as missionaries, so they needed to procure employment. Elise organised a library and earned an MA while helping to begin a linguistics department at the local university. It was 'easily very busy,' but team life faltered. Elise and her team went to a western church in English, which was well attended. In contrast, few local believers met together for fellowship.

Ten years later, Elise moved to London, a 'great place to work' with its large Muslim communities. Initially, she worked with Operation Mobilisation among students and taught Islamics to various groups and at London Bible College and London School of Theology. For seven years she was a hospital chaplain, while continuing to mentor Christian believers who had come out of Islam. She also learned to 'help people die' well, aided by her lead pastor. It was a 'surprise experience,' but she 'loved it.' Elise has been a mission partner at All Souls church since she arrived in London.

Elise has remained single. Once or twice, people said to her single missionaries should be 'good babysitters.' Over the years, several American missionaries told Elise women should not teach. She became used to it, but they were not kind and sometimes she was aggrieved.

Marnie

When two hundred naval servicemen from the Arabian Peninsula spent two and a half years in Marnie's small Scottish village with one traffic light, her eyes were opened. God gave her 'love for and interest in my heart' for Arab Muslims.

Some family members tried to talk Marnie out of living in the Middle East, expressing concern for her safety. She has not regretted her decision, 'not once!' However, there were days when Marnie felt like quitting, when 'only her call (which was so clear)' kept her there.

Seeing how the Lord changes people has been a privilege for Marnie. Nothing compares with seeing 'lives transformed after [receiving] Jesus.' She is part of a team that sells Bibles and other literature and she considers it a joy when Arab Muslims buy Bibles.

Life has its challenges, including living in a country where Marnie is not able to freely share her faith and locals are not allowed to receive. It is hard to disciple and encourage believers who fear their family's reaction or whose 'families have already rejected them.' Marnie also finds her identity to be a challenge, as she is in the Middle East in response to God's call, but in front of her friends, she is simply working at a bookshop.

Singleness gives Marnie flexibility as she does not have to 'juggle family and ministry' and her attention is focused on her ministry. She does not have to 'work around a husband's calling, wants, and preferences,' and has room and freedom to share her house with guests.

Not being able to depend on a husband has made Marnie rely on the Lord and trust him more. Being single means she has done things she might not have otherwise done with someone else to rely on, thus building 'strength and confidence.' Because Marnie has more time to invest in the local culture, she feels she has been accepted in sweet and cherished relationships.

Not being married also has its cons. People try to match Marnie up, particularly others in the church. Some Muslim women are 'suspicious,' wondering why she is in the Arab world. There is a 'constant pressure' in the host culture, where it is not good to be single.

Marnie has been inspired by reading about missionaries like Samuel Zwemer, Tom Hamblin, Joy Loewen, and George Verwer.

The Scripture that confirmed God's call on Marnie was Genesis 21:17–20, the account of God's compassion for Hagar and Ishmael. She is helped by the Bible passages that remind us of God's promises for Arabia. Marnie also cites Isaiah 40:31, Lamentations 3:22–23, Philippians 4:19, Colossians 4:3–4 and Psalm 126:5–6.

Gemma

When 'God grabbed me' for Muslim ministry at a student conference, 'I was hooked,' writes Gemma. With 970 million Muslims, she learned that missionaries among them were one in a million. Gemma has not regretted her decision. She has considered quitting to work in a grocery store frequented by Arabs. 'Ah, to live a "normal" life,' she muses.

Gemma's observant Catholic family in the US did not comprehend evangelism, fundraising, nor her call, but they did not stop her. Church friends view Gemma as fearless, but she shies away, as that implies Muslims are frightening. When she later lived in Beirut, bomb explosions prompted letters of concern, provoking Gemma to 'cheekily' enquire about homicides state-side that weekend.

Gemma's initial exposure to the spiritual needs of the Muslim world occurred during a visit to Turkey. During that time, the Lord called her to 'learn about and love Muslims in the name of Jesus' and assist

Christians to do the same. She went on to enroll in a seminary where she linked churches with mosques to improve mutual understanding. This was followed by two exciting years in London at a friendship centre in a Moroccan neighbourhood. Gemma remains in contact with some of those girls, who are now married with children, and who still recall the songs and stories from the Bible. The team served countless meals and had endless chats with women that 'glorified Jesus, affirmed the worth of the women ... and taught us about what it means to truly be a neighbor.' While Gemma did not see anyone commit themselves to the Lord, she testifies that God will use these seeds and someone else will water them.

Although Gemma's London chapter was tough in some ways, it forged her ministry philosophy that people were more important than programmes or money. She also resolved to root her identity in who she is in Jesus and not what she does for Jesus. Issues from her family of origin took Gemma into a season of counselling and healing and subsequently into a new start. God promised to bless the second half of Job's life, and this became Gemma's promise also.

Gemma admitted to her counsellor she was bored and craved 'intellectual stimulation.' She was tired of talking to Arab women about losing and gaining weight, 'singleness/childlessness, food/recipes... aaaarrggghhh!' A surprise reunion with a seminary tutor resulted in Gemma entering a doctoral program, where she considered herself to be a 'thoughtful practitioner rather than an academic.' Throughout this leg of her journey, she witnessed God's generosity.

Being single means Gemma is freer, and has a 'flexibility' that might be missing if she was married. After a recent surgery, though, Gemma wished for a husband to 'dote' on her. She is on her own but is not alone and has put effort, time, and many miles into maintaining friends who are like family.

Being single in ministry to Arabs has its challenges, who think it is not normal to be single once you reach a certain age. Gemma does begin to wonder what is wrong with her, but seeks to contradict the queries with the way God sees her. This can lead to speaking of waiting for her Father in heaven to 'arrange my marriage.'

Gemma is inspired by examples from the past like Amy Carmichael, Lilias Trotter, and Jim Elliott. She is also inspired by Margaret Higgs, a cheerful retired missionary. Gemma does not want to be a 'sourpuss old broad.'

Inspiration for Gemma invariably comes from Habakkuk 3:17-19. Notably, Job 42 and Psalm 1 face each other in the text of the Bible. God blessed the second half of Job's life more than the first. Gemma aspires to be that tree planted beside the water with deep roots, fruit, and green leaves.

Bethany

When God first began to speak to Bethany about ministering overseas, Bethany wasn't sure where it would be specifically. Over time, she thought God was directing her to North Africa where she had served for several years, however the Lord kept taking her to the Middle East where she is now. The process was not easy, but easy is not what God promises. He did promise not to forsake, Bethany maintains.

No one tried to talk Bethany out of going overseas, but her sending agency did encourage her to ask her family for their blessing. So, Bethany's mom underlined 2 Timothy 4:1-5 and signed it, 'Do the work of an evangelist, fulfil your ministry. Love, Mom.' Bethany did seek the Lord about returning home to the US when some family members faced significant medical challenges. Friends have not understood why she has remained overseas, but she only owes an answer to the Lord.

While Bethany has not regretted going overseas, it has not been easy to be away from her family whom she loves dearly. It is tough to miss times of joy and sorrow or be absent when her family is struggling. Bethany has played the game of 'what if,' but God has been faithful and makes no mistakes. Her job is to obey.

Bethany perseveres in sharing truth and being a link in a chain. One of her greatest joys is sharing Bible stories with local friends, who then ask for a Bible. One woman told Bethany she had been 'waiting for someone to ask about getting a Book.' These women risk danger from their families if they take a Bible, so follow-up is not always possible. When local friends see Bethany's 'confidence and joy' in Christ, they have said, 'I want what you have and I don't know how' to get it.

Along with her colleagues, Bethany hosts Christmas and Easter celebrations where they share from the Bible. On more than one occasion, her friends spontaneously repeat these stories the following year. God is using them to share the Good News.

One of Bethany's challenges is seeing how deeply Islam is entrenched. She and her colleagues continue to share but have seen few respond. Others have declared themselves to be Christians, only to disappear as discipleship begins. Their families may have stopped them and it is hard to tell if they are continuing to pursue the Lord or not. Bethany does pray for them, which is potent.

Another challenge is when Bethany is about to meet a local friend, only for them to cancel. She seeks to channel these frustrations into a reminder of God's grace towards her.

Being single does have its advantages. Through many transitions overseas, Bethany does not have to be concerned how this might affect her family life. She is also free to pursue relationships and not have to consider someone else's schedule. Women feel freer to share with Bethany, as there is no chance she will break their confidence. Singleness is not understood in the Arab world, yet it can be an opportunity to share that it is Christ who completes her. Even if she married, Christ would be the one who completed her, maintains Bethany.

On difficult days, according to Bethany, it would be nice to have someone at home to share with, but 'I've had no one.' This prompts her to depend on her Heavenly Father for his wise comfort. The Lord has brought Bethany lovely friends who have listened and offered support.

Bethany has been inspired by Corrie ten Boom, Amy Carmichael, and Elisabeth Elliot. She did hear Elisabeth Elliot speak twice, but has been mostly inspired by her books.

Scriptures that have been a help are 2 Corinthians 4 and Acts 20:24. She often reads the Psalms for comfort.

Carrie

From a small town in the Canadian Prairies to the throbbing cities of the Middle East, Carrie has come a long way.

Carrie's first foray into the Arab world was to Yemen, where she studied Arabic. She is now farther north in the Gulf and is still pursuing Arabic. She does this by self-study and by sitting with local women. While conversation topics vary, Carrie was thrilled to meet a woman who is eager to study the Bible. This friend enthusiastically downloaded the Word app and asked for an Arabic Bible. She and Carrie have been meeting weekly for a few years to read, joined by her friend's sister. The sisters have witnessed the Lord answering some prayers and have acknowledged the Lord's hand.

Praying with local friends is a highlight of Carrie's ministry. She was initially nervous, but sees her friends' gratitude. When a local friend was particularly upset, Carrie put her arm around her and prayed for her. 'It was a really special moment for both of us,' Carrie writes.

One of the most difficult things in ministry is to meet women who show interest, but do not find time to meet. Carrie has shared with other women who are keen, but lose focus and fade away, leaving Carrie wondering if she was too open or misspoke. Most of her local friends hesitate to be transparent, which makes deeper connections difficult.

Being single means Carrie is freer and more available to visit friends. There is no need to be home to put children to bed. She has the time and space to bake, receive visitors or help others on her team. She also has time to study Arabic, which is a building block for establishing genuine friendships.

Singleness has its pros and cons. If Carrie was married, she could more easily relate to the husbands of her friends. If she had children, she could connect with those with children. On the other hand, she could not relate as well to those who are not married or do not have children.

Carrie does not feel that being single hampers her ministry, but there are other implications. Putting together furniture and dealing with utilities are all up to her. Also, no one person is a 'witness to my whole adult life.' She does not have someone who has been with her in Canada and the Arab world, 'who is there for all the celebrations and losses.' Instead, she has a variety of friends and people she knows for a time.

Carrie continues to be inspired by Marilyn, a former team leader, with whom she remains in contact. Marilyn first began to tackle Arabic in her 50s and became near and dear to a number of Arab families. Carrie admires that Marilyn moved away from her home and family to follow the Lord's call, sometimes in 'very challenging circumstances.'

Advice from the Current Crop

A word of advice to single women from single women in ministry in the Arab world.

Nora

It is not easy. Yet, it is not difficult when God is in it.

Speak to women/sisters who are living in the Arab world to gain a feel and flavour of where you might fit in best. Utilise your time off to conduct survey trips or join a short term team. For nursing, midwifery, and medical students, try to secure an elective in the Arab world.

Language learning is important, but I would not say 100% a necessity. Expose yourself to the language to see if you can manage to learn it.

If you are desperate to marry, do not expect to come and find a husband easily. Statistically there are not as many brothers as sisters on the field.

Living in the Arab world needs loads of flexibility and can be highly stressful at first. So, learn about your coping mechanisms and how you de-stress.

You really need the support of your church, pastor, accountability partners, and church family. Join a sending organisation, because they have the expertise to help support you, as part of a three-way relationship with your church.

Pray for peace and for the open door, which is the most obvious thing.

Marnie

Be clear about your calling, as many days that may be the only thing you hold onto.

Ask God to give you the same love for the people that He has.

Nurture a prayer support group at home.

Do a course on spiritual warfare as part of your preparation. Prepare also by reading about Arab culture and start learning the language. View the host nation/culture as being different not as being bad. Respect their culture instead of trying to change it or speak out against it. Rather than tackling the differences, try to find common ground.

Adhere to the dress code.

Be willing to be flexible as plans continually change.

Gemma

I suggest everyone interested in working with Muslims—Arab or not—is to study Arabic first, even before Islam, even if you are working with Persians, Turks, or Bangladeshis. Understanding Arabic is the key that unlocks so much about Islam and Muslim cultures and worldview.

Do not trade God's best for what you think is better! Do not be tempted to marry someone who is not right for you just to fit in or to meet someone else's expectations. I would much rather be fifty-eight and single than married to the wrong man.

Acknowledge that the American Evangelical church has made an idol out of marriage and family, which is not a biblical picture of family. Build a family around you of mothers, fathers, brothers, sisters, nieces and nephews of your choosing. Work hard at being a faithful friend with those people.

Keep things in perspective. Being single is hard. Being married is hard.

Life on earth is a blip. Life on the New Earth is forever. And we are going to be single forever on the New Earth.

If you are not joyful and content as a single person, it may be hard to be joyful and content as a married person. Gratitude is the foundation of joy and contentment. Be thankful.

Listen to what God says about you, not about what anyone else says about you. Build your sense of worth, identity, and confidence on the solid bedrock of God's truth. Work hard at turning down the volume of your own inner critic.

Cultivate intimacy with Jesus. Daily.

Ask for help when you need it. Learn emotionally-healthy ways of articulating what you need and also what you want. Do not try to be a superwoman. Know what you are good at and what you are not good at. Unapologetically live with that.

Figure out what you have control over and what you do not. If you want to be married and have the opportunity to be in a situation where you will meet more prospects, go for it! But, as a wise friend of mine told me years ago, 'Gemma, put your hand to the plow and serve the Lord. Every once in a while, look up and see if there's anyone interesting working there too . . . if not, put your hand back to the plow and keep trusting the Lord.'

God sees (Hagar) and God knows (Hannah). His love for you runs deep. Trust Him.

Do not repress your emotions regarding singleness and marriage. Learn how to be honest with yourself, your friends, and supporters (in appropriate ways!) and most importantly with Jesus about how you're feeling.

Deal with the grief. Celebrate the joys. Recently I had a most powerful encounter with this grief. I was at the wedding of a young couple, friends from church. Weddings are not as hard for me now as they were in my 20s, 30s, and 40s. So, I was completely caught off guard during the reception when the mother of the groom joined her son for their special dance. My throat tightened and tears threatened to spill over . . . I felt the acute sorrow of never having a son to dance with at his wedding! I am tempted to say this 'came out of nowhere,' but it comes out of the reality that as unmarried people we live with unfulfilled dreams and unmet hopes that may be latent, but very real and very much a part of us.

Throw a huge party for every birthday ending in '0.' Don't fret getting older. Great things come with age.

Stay physically healthy. I use food way too often to stuff everything down. I am still committed to the truth that ultimately the scale measures my weight, not my worth, and I will fight against societal standards of 'beauty.' I realise now that while I could carry extra weight in my early years, it has caught up with me and caused numerous physical limitations. It is a huge regret and a challenge I am constantly working through.

Cultivate interests and hobbies that have nothing to do with church/ministry. Be a well-rounded person! Read more than watch. Move more than sit.

Bethany

If you are not already disciplining yourself daily by spending time reading the Word and in prayer, start now before you come to the field. No matter where you are or who you are, you need that intentional time with God.

If there is anything in your life that you have not yet dealt with, whether it be a sin issue or an emotional issue, confront it before you come overseas. Do not think that jumping on a plane is going to separate you from your problems.

Any right you think belongs to you, lay it down at the foot of the cross.

Remember that passion God gave you to proclaim the gospel to the people you are coming to serve. On days where you are having a hard time loving them, or those you are working with, remember how God first loved you. Preach the gospel to yourself daily.

Seek the fellowship of other believers when you arrive on the field. Do not ever think you are so spiritual or so strong that you do not need accountability. Not only do we need to continually preach the truth to ourselves, but we need others to do this as well. However, do not come and hang out only with other believers and not locals. I have watched too many people fall into this trap, where they spend more time with other like-minded expats than with the people they claimed to be called to.

Carrie

It is not as scary as you might think! I truly feel safer walking alone in my adopted city than I do in cities in Canada. Most men here are very respectful towards women.

Be part of a team, whether officially or unofficially, one that fosters community. My team was composed of only two others when I arrived. Others have come and gone, but at the moment my team has been the same for two years in a row. My team has made all the difference in how quickly I adapted to life here and to my level of thrivingness (yup, just made that up). Location is secondary to being part of a connected team. Seek out a team that you connect with! Visit other teams if possible.